The Complete Works of William Shakespeare

William Shakespeare

(abridged) [revised] [again]

The Complete Works of William Shakespeare

(abridged) [revised] [again]

Adam Long, Daniel Singer, and Jess Winfield

New Revisions by Jess Winfield and Daniel Singer

APPLAUSE
THEATRE & CINEMA BOOKS
Essex, Connecticut

THEATRE & CINEMA BOOKS
An imprint of Globe Pequot, the trade division of
The Rowman & Littlefield Publishing Group, Inc.
4501 Forbes Blvd., Ste. 200
Lanham, MD 20706
www.rowman.com

Distributed by NATIONAL BOOK NETWORK

Library of Congress Cataloging-in-Publication Data
Names: Long, Adam, author. | Singer, Daniel, author. | Winfield, Jess,
   author.
Title: The complete works of William Shakespeare (abridged) [revised]
   [again] / Adam Long, Daniel Singer, and Jess Winfield.
Description: Essex, Connecticut : Applause Theatre & Cinema Books, 2023.
Identifiers: LCCN 2023026696 | ISBN 9781493077304 (paperback) |
   ISBN 9781476850566 (electronic)
Subjects: LCSH: Shakespeare, William, 1564-1616—Adaptations.
Classification: LCC PR2877 .L85 2023 | DDC 822.3/3—dc23/eng/20230710
LC record available at https://lccn.loc.gov/2023026696

The Complete Works of William Shakespeare (abridged) was first performed (more or less in its entirety) by the authors on June 19, 1987, at the Paramount Ranch in Agoura, California, and subsequently at the 1987 Edinburgh Festival Fringe. Additional premieres with different casts include the Arts Theatre, London (1992), the Westside Theater Off-Broadway (1995), and the Criterion Theatre in London's West End (1996).

A revised version—*The Complete Works of William Shakespeare (abridged) [revised]*—was completed in 2007 and published in 2011.

Notes

PLAYWRIGHTS' NOTE: The script is written for three actors. Where Shakespearean characters appear in the script, the character name is preceded by the actor's initial: e.g, A/JULIET means Adam is playing Juliet, D/ROMEO means Daniel is playing Romeo, J/HAMLET means Jess is playing Hamlet, etc. In performance, the actors should substitute *their own* names and pronouns for those of JESS, ADAM, and DANIEL.

More or less Shakespearean dialogue appears in double quotation marks (" "). Care should be taken to speak it accurately—unless it's for a laugh.

ALSO NOTE: Because the show comments on contemporary events to place Shakespeare's works in a modern context, it's absolutely essential to keep the show fresh and timely by updating the many topical references as events warrant. For example, the default *Desperate Housewives* riff in act two might be replaced by equivalent dialogue referring to any currently popular sappy soap opera or guilty-pleasure reality show. It has, in various incarnations, been *thirtysomething*, *Melrose Place*, *Ally McBeal*, *General Hospital*, and *Twilight*. Also, please, have some fun and come up with your very own put-downs of annoying powerful people where required.

ALSO ALSO NOTE: Far be it from us writers to tell you directors and actors how to stage the show; but having performed it ourselves about a zillion times, we thought we'd offer you a smidgen of performance advice.

The show was developed through improvisation and ad lib, and is predicated on the conceit that this is the first performance ever of this play and the three actors are making much of it up as they go along, getting by on enthusiasm and boundless energy wherever they lack talent or any real clue about Shakespeare's work. It's important that the actors be genuinely surprised by each line, each action, and each turn of events. For example, although the audience participation section of act two is presented here based on our broad experience with how audiences generally respond, each audience is different. The actors should respond honestly to the audience's performance, and their own, rather than stick blindly to the written text. The whole show should feel so spontaneous that the audience will never really know if that screaming audience member was a plant (she wasn't), if Daniel really stepped on Adam's crotch in *Romeo and Juliet* (he didn't), or if Jess really watches *Desperate Housewives* (no, he prefers *Survivor*).

Above all, have fun.

And do it *FASTER!*

Act One

The set consists of a low-budget representation of an Elizabethan theater in the fashion of Shakespeare's Globe, with four escapes: upstage right and left, and downstage right and left. Treads allow easy access between the stage and the audience. A wooden bookstand dead center bears a large book: The Complete Works of William Shakespeare. *Big orchestral music—the finale to 'Jupiter, Bringer of Jollity' from Gustav Holst's* The Planets—*reaches its crashing climax as the preset fades to black. Lights come up on the stage to reveal DANIEL in business casual attire, ostensibly house staff for the theater.*

[*NOTE: If there are any additional announcements to be made before the performance, they should be made by DANIEL as part of this opening speech.*]

DANIEL: Hello, and welcome to this performance of *The Complete Works of William Shakespeare (abridged).* I have just a few brief announcements before we get underway. The recording of this performance by any means—photo, audio, or video—is strictly prohibited. If you have a mobile phone, please take a moment now to turn it off. Trust me, you really don't want to mess with our 'zero-tolerance policy.'

For your convenience, toilets are located in the bathroom.

Now that that's out of way, we can get on with *The Complete Works of William Shakespeare*—right after you agree to our Terms of Service. No need to read it. It's the usual liability waiver, criminal record affidavit, next of kin, blah blah blah. To sign it electronically, just take your forefinger and place it on your arm, on the spot where you were last vaccinated. If you're not vaccinated, raise your hand and an 'usher' will gladly inject you with a tracking chip. Don't worry, it's a small one.

Allow me to introduce myself. My name is Daniel Singer. When I was in kindergarten, I saved up my pennies and this [*Picking up the book.*] is the first thing I bought. This—for those of you who have never seen one before—is a *book.* [*Opens cover, leafs through pages.*] Ink, printed on sheets of paper, bound in leather. No battery. No touchscreen. You can't take a selfie with it. It is simply a book. But not just any book. It's *The Complete Works of William Shakespeare*, which, for me, is the best book in the history of books. Sure, it's violent and racist and sexist and jingoistic and patriarchal. But it's no worse on those fronts than the Bible. And the plots make a lot more sense. And there's even more cross-dressing, so . . . definitely better.

Now, this strange room that you are all sitting in is called a 'theater.' It's the place where the words in this book come to life. Where the magic happens. Ah, the history of the [*Name of theater*]. Who can forget that one-night-only staged reading of *American Psycho: The Musical*? Or the Sunday matinee when Spongebob had a major costume malfunction of his squarepants?

[*The above can be customized to suit the unique history of this theater.*]

And now, tonight, in this very theater . . . the stage manager tells us we have to be out in two hours.

Seriously, we got a good deal on rent but there's a guy doing an adult puppet show in the late slot, and he's already backstage and he scares me.

But fear not—although the time we have is short, the feat we will attempt is impossible. Tonight, my partners and I will attempt to capture the magic, the genius, the towering grandeur of THE COMPLETE WORKS OF WILLIAM SHAKESPEARE!

[*Assessing the weight of the book.*] Now, we've got a lot to get through tonight. So without further ado, I'd like to introduce an individual who knows more about Shakespeare than anyone he knows. One of [*Insert name of region*]'s most preeminent Shakespearean scholars, he has a Bachelor's Degree from [*Insert name of university*] and a Certificate of Completion from preëminentshakespeareanscholar.com. Please welcome me in joining Mr. Jess Winfield.

[JESS *enters in trendy garb and spectacles—he wants to come across as an intellectual, but he's trying a little too hard. He shakes hands with* DANIEL, *who hands him the book and steps far stage left to listen.*]

JESS: Thank you, Daniel, and good evening, friends. [*Hugging the* Complete Works *book too lovingly, he begins professorially, as if lecturing a class of students.*] William Shakespeare: Playwright, poet, actor; Stratford's proudest flower, transplanted from the heart of the English countryside to bask in the warmth of London's literary greenhouse. A man who, despite the ravages of male pattern baldness, planted the potent seed of his poetical genius in the fertile womb of Elizabeth's England. There it took root and spread through the lymphatic system of western civilization, until it became a giant carbuncle of knowledge and understanding on the very organ of our consciousness.

DANIEL: [*At a loss for words.*] Wow.

JESS: And yet, how much do we intellectually flaccid members of the twenty-first century appreciate the plump fruit of Shakespeare's loins?

DANIEL: Yeah—how much?

JESS: Let's find out, shall we? [*To the light booth.*] Bob, may I have the house lights, please?

[*The house lights come up.*]

Now, you are a theater-going crowd, obviously of above-average literary intelligence, and yet—if I may have just a brief show of hands, how many of you have ever seen or read any play by William Shakespeare? Any contact with the Bard whatsoever, just raise your hands . . . [*Almost everyone raises a hand.*]

[JESS *takes two slow steps backward, then rushes to* DANIEL *in a panic.*]

JESS: [*Sotto.*] We're screwed.

DANIEL: Why?

JESS: I think they know more than we do.

DANIEL: But you're an eminent Shakespeare scholar!

JESS: No, I'm *pre*-eminent.

DANIEL: Then be preëminent.

JESS: Right. [*Regaining his confidence,* JESS *comes back downstage. To audience.*] Okay. How many of you have ever seen or read *All's Well That Ends Well?*

[*Perhaps one-third of the audience raises their hands.* JESS *turns to* DANIEL, *and they exchange a thumbs-up.*]

JESS: [*To audience, confidently.*] Well, that seems to be separating the wheat from the chaff rather nicely. Let's see if we have any *super*-eminent Shakespeare scholars in the house. Has anybody ever seen or read *King John? King John,* anyone?

[ADAM, *sitting in the audience, raises his hand.*]

You have, really? Have you seen it, or read it?

ADAM: Well . . . I downloaded it.

JESS: Would you mind telling us what it's about?

ADAM: It's . . . about a hunchback?

JESS: Would you stand up, please? [ADAM *rises.*] My friends, *ecce homo.*

ADAM: Whoa, not cool!

JESS: Judging by your obvious lack of fluency in Latin, may I presume that you have not matriculated?

ADAM: Well, not today.

JESS: My friends, look at this sad individual. Abandoned by our educational system, hopped up on empty gigabytes of pirated text. And now, look at the person sitting next to you. Go ahead! Look at them! Do you recognize the same vapid expression? The same pores, clogged with the acne of intellectual immaturity? Or do you perhaps see—*keep looking!*—do you see there a longing, a desperate plea for literary salvation?

ADAM: Can I sit down?

JESS: *No!* [*Getting really worked up.*] You stand there before us as a living symbol of a society whose capacity to comprehend, much less attain, the genius of a William Shakespeare has been systematically stunted by *Star Wars* sequels, ravaged by *Real Housewives*, and bankrupted by the babbling blather of Big Brothers and Bachelorettes.

[*JESS is now ignoring* ADAM, *who resumes his seat.* JESS *is now in full-on fire-and-brimstone mode.*]

My people, I say to you, toss out your tawdry television to savor the splendors of the sonnet! Exchange the isolation of the iPhone for the idylls of the iamb! Imagine a world where manly men wear pink tights with pride!

DANIEL: Hallelujah!

JESS: A brave new world, where this book [*Raising* The Complete Works *to the heavens.*] is found in every hotel room in the world!

DANIEL: Amen!

JESS: This is my dream, friends, and it begins here, tonight. Join us in taking the first steps down the path to literary salvation . . . by texting SHAKESPEARE IS GOD to 37154. Standard rates apply. Now on with the show, and may the Bard be with you!

[*The house lights fade as* DANIEL *shakes* JESS's *hand.* JESS *returns the book to* DANIEL *and exits.*]

DANIEL: [*Putting the book back on the bookstand.*] Those of you who own a copy of this book know that no collection is complete without a brief biography of the life of William Shakespeare. Providing this portion of the show will be the third and final member of our company. Please welcome to the stage Mr. Adam Long.

[ADAM *comes to the stage, carrying a smartphone. As he shakes hands with* DANIEL, *he drops his phone. He scrambles to pick it up and starts swiping madly to find his place on the phone.* DANIEL *retires to his corner.*]

ADAM: [*Greets the audience.*] Hey, y'all. [*Indicating the phone.*] Okay, um . . . [*Still swiping.*] I Googled Shakespeare's life so I could tell you all the stuff he did . . . As you can see, I'm not an audience member. I totally punked you. [*Finds place on phone.*] Okay . . . sorry, new phone. [*Holds up phone for audience to see.*] The new [*Insert name of latest flagship smartphone.*] from T-Mobile, a truly tremendous device—

[DANIEL *clears his throat aggressively.*]

ADAM: Okay . . . [*Reading from phone.*] William Shakespeare. William Shakespeare was born in 1564 in the town of Stratford-upon-Avon, War-wick-shy-ur. [*Swipes.*] The third of eight children, he was the eldest son of John Shakespeare, a locally prominent merchant, and Mary Arden, daughter of a Roman. [*Swipes.*] Catholic member of the landed gentry. In 1582, he married Anne Hathaway.

[ADAM *is confused and looks to* DANIEL.]

DANIEL: Different Anne Hathaway.

ADAM: That's a shame. [*Reads.*] Shakespeare arrived in London in 1588. [*Swipes but doesn't find his place; swipes again.*] There, with his provincial charm and folksy wit, he quickly became a popular figure around the U.S. Capitol. [*Stops. Swipes back to double-check. Swipes forward again.*] After dominating Michael Douglas in a debate, winning the highest office in the land, and totally nailing his role in *Bill and Ted's Excellent Adventure* . . . [*Swipes, hesitates.*] . . . Shakespeare issued the Emancipation Proclamation on New Year's Day 1863, thus freeing the slaves. [*To* DANIEL.] I never knew that before! [DANIEL *gestures to him to wrap it up.* ADAM *reads rapidly.*] Although Shakespeare modernized the economy, won the Civil War, and built a transcontinental railroad, he was sadly assassinated at the Globe Theater in 1864 by an actor with a cannon. [*Swipes.*] He lies buried in a log cabin in Stratford. [*Swipes.*] Although there's also a huge monument to him at the mall. [*To audience.*] Thank you.

[ADAM *bows.* DANIEL *shakes his hand and hurries him offstage.*]

DANIEL: Okaaaay, well! The clock is ticking, Adult Puppet Guy is glaring at me from the wings, and so without further, further ado, we are proud to prevent *The Complete Works of William Shakespeare (abridged)*!

[*Blackout. A pretentious, heavy-metal version of 'Greensleeves' crashes through the sound system. At its conclusion, lights come up to reveal* JESS, *in Shakespearean attire and high-top sneakers, holding the large* Complete Works *book. He opens it and begins reading.*]

JESS: "All the world's a stage,
And all the men and women merely players.
They have their exits and their entrances
And one man in his time plays many parts."

How many parts exactly must one man play? Shakespeare's *dramatis personae* numbers one thousand, two hundred and twenty-two roles—thirty-six in *Romeo and Juliet* alone! *Way* too many. Friar Lawrence? Fine. Tybalt? Sure. But Mercutio? Lady Capulet? Unsightly fat on the Bard's otherwise muscular body of work.

[*Enter* ADAM *and* DANIEL, *also in Elizabethan garb and sneakers, limbering up as if preparing to run a marathon. As* JESS *speaks, he moves the book and bookstand far stage right.*]

Let us therefore begin our shrinkage of Shakespeare's massive canon by rendering the blubber of his greatest romantic tragedy down to the bare essentials of the smooth, supple, teenage romance of *Romeo and Juliet*. Prologue!

ADAM and DANIEL: [*Simultaneously, with exaggerated gestures.*]

"Two households, both alike in dignity,
In fair Verona where we lay our scene,
From ancient grudge break to new mutiny
Where civil blood makes civil hands unclean.
From forth the fatal loins of these two foes
A pair of star-crossed lovers take their life,
Whose misadventured, piteous o'erthrows
Do, with their death, bury their parents' strife."

[ADAM *and* DANIEL *bow, flourish, and exit.*]

JESS: Act one, scene one:
Behold two men in search of imbroglio:
The Capulet, Sampson; the Montague, Benvolio.

[*Enter* ADAM *as* BENVOLIO *and* DANIEL *as* SAMPSON, *striking aggressive poses.*]

Verona's fragile peace shall be undone,
And tragedy begin—with the biting of a thumb.

[JESS *exits.*]

A/BENVOLIO: [*Singing.*] O I like to rise when the sun she rises, early in the morning.

D/SAMPSON: [*Singing simultaneously.*] O a sailor's life is the life for me, how I love to sail o'er the bounding sea . . .

[*They see each other.*]

A/BENVOLIO: [*Aside.*] Ooo, it's him. I'm gonna kill him, beat him up, and kill him again.

D/SAMPSON: [*Aside, simultaneously.*] Ooo, it's him. I hate his guts. I hate his family, hate his dog, hate 'em all.

[*They smile and bow to each other. As they cross to opposite sides of the stage,* D/SAMPSON *bites his thumb at* A/BENVOLIO, *who trips* D/SAMPSON *in return.*]

A/BENVOLIO: "Do you bite your thumb at me, sir?

D/SAMPSON: No sir, I do but bite my thumb.

A/BENVOLIO: Do you bite your thumb at *me*, sir?

D/SAMPSON: No sir, I do not bite my thumb at you, sir, but I do bite my thumb. Do you quarrel, sir?

A/BENVOLIO: Quarrel, sir? No, sir.

D/SAMPSON: But if you do, sir, I am for you. I serve as good a man as you.

A/BENVOLIO: No better.

D/SAMPSON: Yes. Better.

A/BENVOLIO: You lie!"

D/SAMPSON: Down with the Montagues!

A/BENVOLIO: Up yours, Capulet!

[*They fly at each other. Massive fight scene, with intentionally lame fight choreography.* JESS *enters as the* PRINCE.]

J/PRINCE: "Rebellious subjects!"

A/BENVOLIO and D/SAMPSON: [*Simultaneously.*] Oh no, it's the Prince. [*They kneel.*]

[D/SAMPSON *and* A/BENVOLIO *silently mimic the* PRINCE *as he speaks, and poke at each other whenever they get the chance.*]

J/PRINCE: "Enemies to the peace. On pain of torture,
Throw your mistemper'd weapons to the ground,
And hear the sentence of your moved prince."

D/SAMPSON: [*Mocks him, then:*] Buzz-kill.

J/PRINCE: "You, Capulet, shall go along with me.
Benvolio, come you this afternoon
To know our farther pleasure in this case."

A/BENVOLIO: [*To* D/SAMPSON.] Brown-nose!

D/SAMPSON: [*To* A/BENVOLIO.] Ass-hat!

J/PRINCE: Language!

[J/PRINCE and D/SAMPSON *exit.*]

A/BENVOLIO: "O where is Romeo? Saw you him today?
Right glad I am he was not at this fray.
But see, he comes!

[DANIEL *makes a grand entrance as* ROMEO, *wearing a 'Romeo' wig and carrying a rose in his teeth. The effect is intended to be extremely romantic. It's not.*]

Good morrow, coz.

D/ROMEO: Is the day so young?

A/BENVOLIO: But new struck nine.

D/ROMEO: Ay, me. Sad hours seem long.

A/BENVOLIO: What sadness lengthens Romeo's hours?

D/ROMEO: Not having that which, having, makes them short.

A/BENVOLIO: In love?

D/ROMEO: Out.

A/BENVOLIO: Out of love?

D/ROMEO: Out of her favor where I am in love.

A/BENVOLIO: Alas that love, so gentle in his view,
Should be so rough and tyrannous in proof.

D/ROMEO: Alas that love, whose view is muffl'd still,
Should without eyes see pathways to her will."

A/BENVOLIO and D/ROMEO: [*Simultaneously.*] O! [*Then quickly outdoing/
re-interpreting each other, variously, ad lib.*] O. O! Oooo. o. O!

A/BENVOLIO: "Go ye to the feast of Capulets.
There sups the fair Rosaline whom thou so lovest
With all the admired beauties of Verona.
Go thither, and compare her face with some that I shall show.
And I shall make thee think thy swan a crow.

D/ROMEO: None fairer than my love."

A/BENVOLIO: There's free beer.

D/ROMEO: Let's go!

[*Exit* A/BENVOLIO *and* D/ROMEO. JESS *re-enters, flips a couple of pages in the
book.*]

JESS: Now hie we to the house of Capulet
Where Romeo shall meet his Juliet.
And where, in a scene of timeless romance,
He'll try to get laid at a Renaissance dance.

[*Exit* JESS. ADAM *enters as* JULIET, *wearing a wig even sillier than Romeo's. She
dances, humming 'Greensleeves.'* D/ROMEO *enters, sees her, and is immediately smitten.*]

D/ROMEO: "O she doth teach the torches to burn bright.
Did my heart love 'til now? Forswear it, sight.
For I ne'er saw true beauty 'til this night.
[*Taking* A/JULIET'S *hand.*]
If I profane with my unworthiest hand
This holy shrine, the gentle fine is this:
My lips, two blushing pilgrims ready stand
To smooth that rough touch with a tender kiss.

A/JULIET: Good pilgrim, you do wrong your hands too much,
Which mannerly devotion shows in this;
For saints have hands that pilgrims' hands do touch
And palm to palm is holy palmers' kiss.

D/ROMEO: Have not saints lips, and holy palmers too?

A/JULIET: Ay, pilgrim. Lips that they must use in prayer.

D/ROMEO: O then, dear saint, let lips do what hands do.

[D/ROMEO *leans in to kiss* A/JULIET, *but she demurs.*]

A/JULIET: Saints do not move, though grant for prayers' sake.

D/ROMEO: Then move not, while my prayers' effect I take.

[D/ROMEO *lunges at her, trying to embrace and kiss her.* A/JULIET *fights him off through the following.*]

A/JULIET: Then from my lips the sin that they have took.

D/ROMEO: Sin from my lips? O trespass sweetly urged.
Give me my sin again."

ADAM: [*Breaking character, sotto voce.*] Hey! No means no!

DANIEL: [*Out of character, sotto voce.*] But I'm supposed to kiss you!

[*As they continue to struggle.*]

ADAM: Forget it!

DANIEL: It's in the script.

ADAM: It is?

DANIEL: Yes!

ADAM: Well . . . okay.

[*They kiss briefly.*]

A/JULIET: [*Pleasantly surprised.*] Hey, that was both appropriate and consensual! [*Realizes she's off-track.*] I mean, "You kiss by the book." [*Puts a hand to her ear, as if hearing an offstage call.*] Oh, coming, mother!

[ADAM *looks around in a panic, curses under his breath: There is no balcony on the set. Getting an idea, he drags* JESS *out from backstage and climbs on his shoulders, chicken-wars style.*]

D/ROMEO: [*During the business above.*] "Is she a Capulet? Ay, so I fear. The more is my unrest." [*Breaking character, to* ADAM.] What are you doing?

A/JULIET: The Balcony Scene.

D/ROMEO: Ah. "But soft, what light through yonder window breaks?"

A/JULIET: O Romeo, Romeo, wherefore art thou Romeo?
Deny thy father and refuse thy name,
Or if thou wilt not, be but sworn my love,
And I'll no longer be a Capulet.
What's in a name, anyway? That which we call a nose
By any other name would still smell.

[*She is beginning to lose her balance and grip and starts to slide down toward the floor.*]

O Romeo, doff thy name, and for thy name
Which is no part of thee, take all myself.

[*She completely loses her grip and plummets to the floor.* JESS *hurriedly exits.*]

D/ROMEO: I take thee at thy word. Call me but love,
And I shall be new-baptiz'd. Henceforth
I never will be Romeo."

A/JULIET: What did you just say?

D/ROMEO: "Call me but love, and I'll be new baptiz'd. Henceforth—"

[A/JULIET *is momentarily confused by the above line.*]

A/JULIET: Call you butt-love?

D/ROMEO: No—"Call me but *love*—"

A/JULIET: Okay—butt-love. Butt-love, butt-love, butt—

[DANIEL *snatches* ADAM'S *hand aggressively to stop him.*]

A/JULIET: "What man art thou? Art thou not Romeo,
And a Montague?

D/ROMEO: Neither, fair maid, if either thee dislike.

A/JULIET: Dost thou love me then? I know thou wilt say aye,
And I will take thy word. Yet if thou swearest,
Thou mayest prove false. O Romeo, if thou dost love,
Pronounce it faithfully.

D/ROMEO: Lady, by yonder blessed moon, I swear—

A/JULIET: O swear not by the moon!

D/ROMEO: What shall I swear by?

A/JULIET: Do not swear at all. Although I joy in thee,
I have no joy in this contract tonight.
It is too rash, too sudden, too unadvised,
Too like the lightning, which doth cease to be
Ere one can say it lightens.
Good night, good night! As sweet repose and rest
Come to thy heart as that within my breast!

[D/ROMEO's *eyebrows jump at the mention of "breast." He goes down on a knee, beseeching.*]

D/ROMEO: O wilt thou leave me so unsatisfied?

[A/JULIET *sits on* D/ROMEO's *knee, her bosom conspicuously in his face.*]

A/JULIET: What satisfaction canst thou have?"

[D/ROMEO *nestles a cheek into her bosom.*]

Whoa, whoa . . . second base is for second date, sweetie.

"Good night, good night; parting is such sweet sorrow."

[*She exits, blowing a kiss to the love-struck* D/ROMEO.]

Bye, butt-love!

[D/ROMEO *strikes a lovesick pose and sighs.* JESS *enters and consults the book.*]

JESS: Lo, Romeo did swoon with love;
By Cupid he'd been crippl't;
But Juliet had a loathsome coz
Whose loathsome name was Tybalt.

[JESS *exits.* ADAM *enters as* TYBALT, *snarling, carrying two foils.*]

A/TYBALT: "Romeo, the love I bear thee can afford
No better term than this: thou art a villain.
Therefore turn and draw.

D/ROMEO: Tybalt, I do protest, I never injured thee,
But love thee, better than thou can'st devise.

A/TYBALT: Thou wretched boy, I am for you!

[*In three swift moves:* A/TYBALT *throws a foil to* D/ROMEO; D/ROMEO *catches it and closes his eyes in fear, foil extended;* TYBALT *steps forward, neatly impaling himself.*]

A/TYBALT: O I am slain."

[ADAM *unceremoniously bows and exits.* DANIEL *panics and runs to consult silently with* JESS, *who flips hurriedly through several pages of the book.* JESS *points to a place in the book,* DANIEL *nods and exits.*]

JESS: Moving right along—
From Tybalt's death onward, the lovers are curs'd,
Despite the best efforts of Friar and Nurse;
Their fate pursues them, they can't seem to duck it . . .
[*Trying to avoid* that *rhyme:*]
And at the end of act five, they both kick the bucket. [*Exits.*]

[A/JULIET *enters, riding an imaginary horse, humming the 'William Tell Overture.'*]

A/JULIET: "Gallop apace, you fiery-footed steeds,
And bring in cloudy night immediately.
Come civil night! Come night! Come Romeo,
Thou day in night! Come, gentle night!
Come loving, black-brow'd night!"
O night night night night . . .
Come come come come come!"

[*To audience, breaking character.*]

I didn't write it.

[*Back in character.*]

"And bring me my Romeo!"

[DANIEL *enters as the* NURSE. *The fake breasts sewn into her dress are flopping around outside the bodice.*]

D/NURSE: [*Wailing.*] Boo hoo hoo hoo!

A/JULIET: O it is my Nurse. [*Sotto.*] Yo, boobs overboard!

DANIEL: Oops! [*Tucks them back inside.*]

A/JULIET: "Now Nurse, what news?

D/NURSE: Alack the day! He's gone, he's kill'd, he's dead!!

A/JULIET: Can heaven be so envious?

D/NURSE: O Romeo! Who ever would have thought it? Romeo!

A/JULIET: What devil art thou to torment me thus?
Hath Romeo slain himself?

D/NURSE: I saw the wound! I saw it with mine own eyes [*Pulling out a fake boob and pointing at it.*], here, in his manly breast.

A/JULIET: Is Romeo slaughter'd and is Tybalt dead?"

D/NURSE: No, "Tybalt is slain and Romeo banished.
Romeo that kill'd Tybalt, he is banished!

A/JULIET: O God! Did Romeo's hand shed Tybalt's blood?

D/NURSE: It did, it did, alas the day it did." [*Wails hysterically.*] Aaaaa! Aaaaaa!

A/JULIET: O Nurse! O . . . O Nurse? [*But it's no use, D/NURSE can't hear through her sobs.*] Nurse!!!

[D/NURSE *wails continuously while running two loops around* A/JULIET, *then exits.*]

A/JULIET: [*Jerks a thumb after her.*] New meds.

[JESS *enters as* FRIAR LAURENCE, *in a hooded brown monk's robe.*]

O Friar Laurence! Romeo is banished and Tybalt is slain and I could really use some pharmaceutical assistance if you know what I mean.

J/FRIAR: "Take thou this vial, and this distilled liquor drink thou off. And presently though thy veins shall run a cold and drowsy humor."

A/JULIET: [*Takes bottle and drinks.*] O I feel a cold and drowsy humor running through my veins . . . [*Re: The monk's robe.*] Obi-wan.

[J/FRIAR *exits.* A/JULIET *becomes slightly dizzy.*]

A/JULIET: Mm, pretty colors! Uh-oh . . .

[A/JULIET *begins to convulse, jumps into the audience, mimes vomiting on several people in the front row, then returns to the stage.*]

A/JULIET: Ah, I feel much better. [*Collapses suddenly.*]

[D/ROMEO *enters. He sees* A/JULIET *and rushes to her prone body.*]

D/ROMEO: "O no! [*On 'no,' he accidentally stomps on* ADAM's *crotch.* ADAM *clutches his groin in agony.*]
My love, my wife!
Death, that hath suck'd the honey of thy breath,
Hath no power yet upon thy beauty.
O Juliet, why art thou yet so fair?"

A/JULIET: I dunno!

D/ROMEO: "Here's to my love. [*He drinks from* A/JULIET's *poison bottle.*]
O true apothecary! Thy drugs are quick.
Thus, with a kiss . . ."

[D/ROMEO *leans in to kiss* A/JULIET. ADAM *burps a nasty poison-burp, which* DANIEL *finds repellent. He takes another swig from the poison bottle and then kisses* ADAM. ADAM *responds so enthusiastically that* DANIEL *pushes him back down.*]

Geez, no *tongue!*—"I die."

[D/ROMEO *dies.* A/JULIET *wakes up, stretches, scratches her butt and looks around.*]

A/JULIET: [*Cheerful.*] Good morning. Where, O where is my love?
[*She sees him lying at her feet, and screams ridiculously loudly.*]
Aaaaaaaaaaaaaaa! "What's this? A cup, closed in my true love's hand?
Poison I see hath been his timeless end. O churl,
Drunk all and left no friendly drop to help me after?
Then I'll be brief. O happy dagger! This is thy sheath."

[*She unsheathes* D/ROMEO'S *dagger and does a double-take: The blade is tiny. To audience.*]

That's Romeo for ya.

[*She stabs herself. She screams, but, to her surprise, she does not feel injured. She looks for a wound but can't find one. Finally she realizes that the blade is retractable. This is a cause for much joy. She stabs herself gleefully in the torso, on the crown of the head, on her butt, up her nostril. She finally flings the happy dagger to the ground.*]

"There rust and let me die!" [*Dies.*]

[JESS *enters with a guitar.*]

JESS: Epilogue!

[JESS *strikes a power chord on the guitar, then plays the famous theme from Zeffirelli's* Romeo and Juliet *as* DANIEL *recites the Epilogue and* ADAM *interprets with absurdly intricate gestures.*]

DANIEL: "A glooming peace this morning with it brings;
The sun for sorrow will not show its head;
Go forth and have more talk of these sad things;
Some shall be pardon'd, and some punished;

For never was there a story of more woe
Than this of Juliet and her Romeo."

ALL: [*Singing, to the theme's finale.*] And Romeo and Juliet are dead!

[*They rock out, jamming a rock 'n' roll coda, ending with all three doing a synchronized Pete Townshend-style jump on the last chord.*]

[*Blackout. Lights come back up. The actors are having a discussion among themselves.*]

DANIEL: Okay! So we did *R and J* in twelve minutes.

JESS and ADAM: Awesome!

DANIEL: Not awesome. At this rate, *The Complete Works* will take seven hours.

JESS and ADAM: Crap!

ADAM: I have an idea! Let's give up.

JESS: Not an option. We'll just have to keep 'em super short. Daniel, read this intro. [*Hands him an index card, grabs ADAM, and they exit.*]

DANIEL: [*Starts reading from card.*] In approaching Shakespeare's cruder early work, Jess has delved into the Bard's jejune carnal impulses, manifested in the context of the agrarian-dash-urban demographic shift in late-Renaissance-slash-early-modern England. So here's Shakespeare's first tragedy, *Titus Andronicus*, as a cooking show!

[*A brief, cheesy musical sting brings on JESS as TITUS ANDRONICUS, an aggressive celebrity chef, wearing an apron and carrying a large butcher's knife. He has a bloody stump where his left hand should be.*]

J/TITUS: Hello, and welcome to another delicious episode of *Kitchen Tragedies!* I'm your host, Titus Andronicus—a.k.a The Gory Gourmet.
Now, when you've had a crappy day—your left hand chopped off, your sons murdered, your daughter raped, her tongue cut out, and both her hands chopped off—well the last thing you want to do is cook! Unless you cook up the rapist and serve him to his sick, twisted tyrant of a mother at a dinner party. My daughter Lavinia and I will show you how.

[ADAM *enters as* LAVINIA, *carrying a large mixing bowl between her two stumps and kicking* DANIEL, *as the* RAPIST, *forward in front of her.* DANIEL *mimes having his hands bound behind his back.*]

Hello, Lavinia. Are you as enraged as I am?

A/LAVINIA: [*Deep, primal scream/growl.*]

J/TITUS: Ready to bake up some sweet revenge?

A/LAVINIA: [*Even deeper, more primal scream/growl.*]

[A/LAVINIA *kicks* D/RAPIST *to his knees, facing upstage.*]

J/TITUS: "Then hark, villain. I will grind your bones to dust,
And of your blood and it I'll make a paste;
And of the paste a coffin I will rear
And make a pasty of your shameful head.
Come, Lavinia, receive the blood."

[A/LAVINIA *holds the bowl underneath* D/RAPIST'S *throat to collect the 'blood.'*]

First of all, we want to make a nice, clean incision from carotid artery to jugular vein, like so. [*Slices* D/RAPIST'S *throat with knife.*]

D/RAPIST: Aaaaargh!

[D/RAPIST *convulses and the bowl fills with 'blood.' Easy way to do this:* ADAM *pulls* DANIEL's *red cloth cap off his head and into the translucent bowl, and swirls it around.*]

A/LAVINIA: [*Joyous, cackling, vengeful laugh.*]

J/TITUS: Oh, this is satisfying, isn't it?

[A/LAVINIA *nods enthusiastically, still CACKLING.*]

J/TITUS: [*To audience:*] Be sure to use a big bowl for this because the human body has about four quarts of blood in it. "And when that he is dead," which should be—

[D/RAPIST *collapses to the floor with a loud thunk.*]

—right about now . . .

[A/LAVINIA *exits, dragging the corpse backstage. We hear short blasts of a chainsaw: starting, then running, then cutting.*]

". . . Let me go grind his bones to powder small,
And with this hateful liquor temper it;
And in that paste let his vile head be baked—"
—at about five hundred degrees, because this revenge is best served FREAKING HOT! And forty minutes later, you have this lovely human head pie—

[A/LAVINIA *re-enters with a truly disgusting-looking pie.*]

—which I prepared earlier. [*Pulls a severed hand from the pie.*] With ladyfingers for dessert! Now, who will play the Empress and taste this dainty, high-protein treat?

[J/TITUS *and* A/LAVINIA *offer the pie to a* WOMAN *in the audience.*]

"Welcome, dread queen.
Will't please you eat?
Will't please you feed?"
It's finger-lickin' good!

[*He licks the bloody severed hand.*]

A/LAVINIA: [*Excited by the clever line.*]

[*They try to give each other a high five, but since neither has a hand, it is a miserable failure. They shoot an angry look at the face in the pie and then pummel it with their stumps and elbows.*]

J/TITUS and A/LAVINIA: [*Angry pummeling sounds.*]

J/TITUS: Does that taste like closure, Lavinia?

A/LAVINIA: [*Happy agreement sounds.*]

J/TITUS: There you go. It's another kitchen catharsis! Be sure to watch our next episode, a two-parter where Coriolanus will share his recipe for Hoarded Cornbread, and we'll see Timon of Athens in a meaty new take on the Greek Salad. Till then, *bone appetit!*

[J/TITUS *and* A/LAVINIA *exit to a musical outro sting.* DANIEL *rises and dusts himself off.*]

DANIEL: Remember, I warned you about all the violent, patriarchal stuff. But let's move on from his earlier, cruder plays to his later work. Adam will now interpret the Bard's more mature treatment of the themes of jealousy, revenge, and betrayal in his dark and brooding tragedy, *Othello, the Moor of Venice.*

[DANIEL *exits. Lights go dim and moody.* ADAM *enters as* OTHELLO, *with plastic boats on a string draped around his neck.*]

A/OTHELLO: "Speak of me as I am; let nothing extenuate
Of one who loved not wisely, but too well:"
For never was there a story of more woe
Than this of Othello and his Desdemono.
[*He stabs himself with a tugboat.*]
O Desi!

[*He dies amid a clatter of plastic boats.*]

[DANIEL *and* JESS *watch in distress from a doorway. They confer briefly, then enter.*]

DANIEL: [*To the light booth.*] Bob, can we have some lights please?

[*Lights come back up.*]

DANIEL: Adam. Oh. My god. That was so embarrassing.

JESS: [*To audience.*] Indeed. It seems that Adam, secure in the infallibility of the Internet, has Googled the word 'Moor' and determined that it's a place where you tie up boats.

ADAM: I didn't Google it, I Wiki'd [*Or ChatGPT'd, or whatever the latest dispenser of digital misinformation might be.*] it.

JESS: Lose the boats.

[ADAM *looks to* DANIEL *for support.* DANIEL *shakes his head.* ADAM *stomps petulantly toward the wing and flings the boats offstage.*]

DANIEL: [*To audience.*] Just curious—how many of you here know what a 'Moor' is? Go on, shout it out.

[*The audience shouts various responses.*]

DANIEL: [*He also has no idea what a Moor is.*] Can you believe these people? Wow. So, Jess, what's a Moor?

JESS: Seriously? [*Shakes his head.*] You know what? I think this is an opportunity for a much-needed deep dive into the important issues of ethnic, 'racial' identity vis-a-vis male/female power dynamics in an arguably white male supremacist society.

DANIEL: [*After a beat.*] I have a better idea! What if the boats were awesome, and we're done with *Othello*?

ADAM: [*Raises a fist in triumph.*] Yes!

JESS: [*Annoyed but compliant.*] Fine.

ADAM: Hey, howzabout we take a little break from all these heavy tragedies and move on to the comedies?

JESS: They *do* have fewer issues with outdated notions of ethnicity.

DANIEL: [*Enthusiastically.*] Not really, but sure!!

ALL: [ALL *raise a fist.*] Comedy!

JESS: [*To audience.*] Shakespeare's comedies were greatly influenced by the Roman plays of Plautus and Terence, Ovid's hilarious *Metamorphoses*, and the rich Italian tradition of *Commedia dell'Arte*. The Bard was a genius at borrowing and adapting plot devices from these different theatrical traditions.

ADAM: Isn't that called 'plagiarism?'

JESS: Shakespeare did not 'plagiarize,' he 'distilled.' [*Exits.*]

ADAM: Whatever. He's a big cheater.

DANIEL: Hey, it takes a real genius to milk five ideas into sixteen plays.

ADAM: Yeah, but I can never tell them apart. Like what's that one with the shipwreck, the identical twins, and the big wedding at the end?

DANIEL: All of them.

ADAM: See, that sucks.

[JESS *re-enters, and distributes three thin manuscripts.*]

JESS: Well, Shakespeare obviously should have written one exemplary play instead of sixteen sucky ones. Which is why I have taken the liberty of condensing Shakespeare's comedic diarrhea into a single, solid, well-formed lump of hilarity, which I have entitled: *The Comedy of Two Well-Measured Gentlemen Lost in the Merry Wives of Venice on a Midsummer's Twelfth Night in Winter.* Or—

DANIEL: [*Reading the cover.*] '*Cymbeline Taming Pericles the Merchant in the Tempest of Love As Much As You Like It For Nothing.*' Or—

ALL: *The Love Boat Goes to Verona!*

[*They read from their manuscripts. NOTE: This may be done reader's theater style, or the scripts may be placed on bookstands, freeing up the actors to use props, masks, puppets, or other devices. But the conceit is that the other two actors are seeing* JESS'S *script for the first time.*]

JESS: Act one! A Bohemian duke swears an oath of celibacy, turns the rule of the city over to his tyrannical brother, and sets sail for the Golden Age of Greece. While rounding the heel of Italy, the duke's ship is caught in a terrible tempest that casts him up on a desert island along with his daughter, a sweet, innocent, clueless young thing with a sick booty!

A/PRINCESS: O dear father, I am so lonely and pubescent on this island! I am sad, boo-hoo. And frisky, rrarr.

D/DUKE: O precious daughter, watch out for hyper-sexualized symbols of colonial oppression lurking in caves!

A/PRINCESS: 'Kay, b-bye!

JESS: Meanwhile, the duke's long-lost son, a handsome, dashing, clueless young merchant, is also shipwrecked—coincidentally, on the very same island.

D/MERCHANT: How shall I survive without funds in this strange, foreign land? I know, I must needs find a moneylender. Behold, here cometh a convenient Judeo-Italian stereotype now.

A/JEW: [*Italian accent.*] Whatsammata you, eh? [*Yiddish accent.*] Need a payday loan, *bubbe*?

JESS: The Jew tricks the merchant into putting down his brains as collateral on the loan.

A/JEW: Such a deal!

JESS: Act two. Fearing ravishment, the clueless young princess disguises herself as a boy and becomes a page to a handsome, dashing, clueless young soldier.

D/SOLDIER: You there, boy!

A/PRINCESS: [*High voice.*] Yes? . . . I mean . . . [*Lowering his voice.*] Yes?

D/SOLDIER: You shall woo Kate for me, for she is shrewish, and I am sick with love and gender dysphoria!

A/PRINCESS: I too feel both phlegmy and confused down there, for while I may not speak it aloud, I do love thee, though I am a boy.

D/SOLDIER: I swingeth not that way, boy. Deliver this letter to Kate the shrew. Go, hence.

A/PRINCESS: Whence?

D/SOLDIER: Hie thee hither from hence to thence!

A/PRINCESS: That doesn't make sense!

D/SOLDIER: Because you're dense.

JESS: The beautiful, clueless young princess arrives in man-drag to woo the shrew.

D/SHREW: It is I, Kate the shrew. I am *so* a woman and you are *totes* a man. Come hither!

A/PRINCESS: Whither?

D/SHREW: Hither, from thither. [*Hitting on her.*] If you come inside, I'll show you my zither.

JESS: Act four. On the Twelfth Night of Midsummer, a puckish sprite leads all the lovers deep into a forest and squeezes the juice of an aphrodisiac flower into their eyes while the queen of the fairies seduces a rude mechanical named Bottom, who coincidentally has the head of an ass.

D/BOTTOM: Yeah, but I have the ass of a man, and I'm hung like a donkey!

JESS: Act five. In the ensuing omnisexual animalistic orgy, the Princess's man-clothes get ripped off, revealing her sick booty . . . and more! The merchant recognizes his sister.

D/MERCHANT: My nearly-identical twin!

A/PRINCESS: My long-lost and strangely attractive brother!

JESS: The shrew realizes she's bi-curious.

D/SHREW: "O Brave New World!"

JESS: The dashing young soldier decides he actually prefers Bottom.

D/SOLDIER: And thereby hangs a sweet tail!

JESS: The Jew exits, pursued by a bear.

A/JEW: Oy!

JESS: And they all get married and live happily ever after. Now give us your hands if we be friends—

ALL: Because all is well that finally ends!

[*They hand their manuscripts to* JESS. JESS *dumps the manuscripts offstage and returns.*]

DANIEL: Sixteen plays in five minutes. Not bad! But if we're gonna get out of here before Adult Puppet Guy starts blowing darts at us, we have to get back to the Tragedies.

ADAM/JESS: [*They give a raised-fist salute.*] Tragedy!

[ADAM *whisks any remaining props/bookstands offstage and re-enters.*]

JESS: Interestingly, we've discovered Shakespeare's comedies aren't nearly as funny as his tragedies.

DANIEL: That is so true. You know what's funny? The Scottish Play.

ADAM: Oh yeah! *Mac—*

DANIEL and JESS: [*Ad lib.*] Sssshhh! Don't say it!

ADAM: Why not?

DANIEL: Because it's cursed. It's bad luck to say the name of that show in a theater unless you're performing it. That's why we refer to it as 'the Scottish Play.'

ADAM: But we *are* performing it. And besides, there's nothing remotely Scottish about it.

JESS: It's all in the performance. It needs to be played so that you can see the heather rippling on the highlands, feel the cold summer breeze wafting up your kilt, and smell the steaming vomit outside the pub.

DANIEL: Good idea. I'll get kilts!

JESS: I'll drink whiskey!

[DANIEL *and* JESS *look expectantly at* ADAM. ADAM *gives the raised-fist salute again.*]

ADAM: Vomit!

DANIEL: With your kind indulgence, we now present our authentically Scottish interpretation of *Macbeth*.

[*Lights darken, and a short blast on the bagpipes is heard, as* DANIEL *becomes a* WITCH.]

D/WITCH: "Double, double, toil and trouble.

[JESS *enters as* MACBETH, *carrying a bag of golf clubs. In nearly impenetrable attempts at Scottish accents:*]

J/MACBETH: Stay, ye imperrrfect MacSpeakerrrrr. MacTell me MacMorrrrre.

D/WITCH: "Macbeth, Macbeth, beware Macduff.
  No man of woman born shall harm Macbeth
  Till Birnam Wood come to Dunsinane, don't ye know.

[D/WITCH *exits.* ADAM *enters as* MACDUFF, *also carrying golf clubs and hiding behind a leafy twig.*]

J/MACBETH: Och, that's daid greeet. Then MacWhat MacNeed MacI MacFearrr Macduff?"

[A/MACDUFF *throws down his disguise, wields a golf club and throws a two-fingered gesture at* J/MACBETH.]

A/MACDUFF: See *you*, ye brah-flocked, nanny-figgish clunge-MacKinley! It's days of Auld Lang Syne fer yew! "Know that Macduff was from his mother's womb untimely ripped!" What d'ye think aboot that?

J/MACBETH: Och! I do nae like it, but I support a woman's right tae choose! Lay on, haggis-breath!

[J/MACBETH *pulls out a golf club, and they fence.*]

A/MACDUFF: Ah, Macbeth! Ye killed me wife, ye murdered me wee bairns, and ye shat in me stew!

J/MACBETH: Och! I didnae!

A/MACDUFF: Och, aye, ye did. I had tae throw half o'it away.

[A/MACDUFF *chases* J/MACBETH *offstage. Backstage,* J/MACBETH's SCREAM *is abruptly cut off with a loud thwack.* A/MACDUFF *re-enters carrying a severed head.*]

A/MACDUFF: "Behold where lies the usurper's cursed head."
Macbeth, yer arse is oot the windee. [*Sets down the head, addresses it like a golf shot, and whacks it into the audience with his club.*]
And know that never was there a story of more blood and death
Than this, o' Mister and Mrs. Macbeth. Thankee. [*Exits.*]

[*End Scottish accents.* JESS *enters.*]

JESS: Meanwhile, in ancient Rome, Julius Caesar was a much beloved tyrant.

[DANIEL *enters as* JULIUS CAESAR, *wearing a laurel wreath.* ADAM *and* JESS *become* CITIZENS.]

A/CITIZEN and J/CITIZEN: All hail, Julius Caesar!

D/CAESAR: Hail, citizens!

JESS: He was warned by a soothsayer—

A/SOOTHSAYER: "Beware the Ides of March."

JESS: The great Caesar, however, chose to ignore the warning.

D/CAESAR: What the hell are the Ides of March?

A/SOOTHSAYER: The 15th of March.

D/CAESAR: Why, that's today.

[ADAM *and* JESS *become* CONSPIRATORS *and stab* D/CAESAR *repeatedly.*]

A/CONSPIRATOR and J/CONSPIRATOR: [*Attacking sounds.*]

D/CAESAR: "Et tu, Brute?

[D/CAESAR *dies.* JESS *becomes* MARK ANTONY, *orating over the body.*]

J/ANTONY: Friends, Romans, countrymen, lend me your ears.
I come to bury Caesar," so bury him, and let's get on to my play, *Antony*—

[ADAM *enters as* CLEOPATRA, *wearing a wig and clutching a rubber snake.*]

A/CLEOPATRA: —*and Cleopatra!* Is this an asp I see before me? Come, venomous wretch—

[A/CLEOPATRA *applies the snake to her breast. A wave of nausea hits her. She leaps into the audience and mimes vomiting on several people in the front row.*]

JESS and DANIEL: Whoa, Adam! No! Stop!

ADAM: What?

DANIEL: You have this bizarre notion that all of Shakespeare's tragic heroines wear really ugly wigs and vomit on people before they die.

ADAM: It's an interpretation.

DANIEL: Barfing is not an interpretation.

ADAM: Even on 'Throw Up Thursday?'

DANIEL: That's not a thing.

JESS: Adam, *Antony and Cleopatra* has nothing to do with gastrointestinal distress. It's a transglobal thriller about political maneuvering across the ancient Mediterranean.

ADAM: Oh, it's one of Shakespeare's transglobal plays? Wow, I love those! Like that one about a transglobal leader in wireless communications that offers two lines with unlimited data for just fifty dollars a month—and did I mention no contracts?

DANIEL/JESS: What?/No!

ADAM: [*Holds up his shiny new device.*] Yeah, it's called 'T-Mobile Kinsmen!' It offers ninety percent nationwide coverage on the nation's best 5G—

JESS: [*Interrupting.*] Adam, Adam!—Shakespeare wrote a play called *The TWO Noble Kinsmen.* Not 'T-Mobile Kinsmen.'

DANIEL and JESS: *TWO Noble Kinsmen.*

ADAM: [*Beat.*] I'm sure it was 'T-Mobile.'

DANIEL: Adam, do you have a product placement deal with T-Mobile?

ADAM: No! They just give me money to mention them and my phone. The [*Insert name of phone.*] really is tremendous.

JESS: *Two Noble Kinsmen* isn't about wireless carriers. It's about two cousins who fall in love with the same woman.

ADAM: And are they all on the Simple Choice family plan?

JESS and DANIEL: No!

ADAM: Well they should be. They could 'Save a Bundle!'

JESS: [*To audience.*] My friends, *Two Noble Kinsmen* falls into the category of Shakespeare's plays which are neither tragedy, comedy, nor history, and which scholars refer to as the 'problem' plays, or in some circles, the 'obscure' plays, or the 'lesser' plays, or simply, the 'bad' plays. And yet, not all of the bad plays are completely without merit. In fact, one of them, *Troilus and Cressida*, is hardly crap at all. I actually discuss it in my unpublished monograph about Shakespeare entitled 'I Love My Willy.' [*Off* ADAM's *and* DANIEL's *reactions:*]

Oh, you two would love it! It's big, it's long, it's uncut, and I've been hammering away on it for years. In fact, if you don't mind, I'd like to whip it out for you right now! [JESS *reaches into his pants.*]

ADAM/DANIEL: Jess!/NO!

JESS: [*Pulls out a manuscript. Then, as if saying, 'What were you expecting?'*] Um, my monograph? [DANIEL *and* ADAM *sigh in relief.*] It has a whole chapter examining authorship markers in the quarto edition of *Troilus* versus the First Folio.

DANIEL: Hey, great—while you read it, maybe we could improvise an interpretive dance, performance art version of your . . . thingy.

ADAM: Oh, I love performance art. It's so . . . pretentious!

DANIEL: Yeah! Get some props!

JESS: Now wait a minute. I was thinking of a more straightforward, scholarly approach.

ADAM: Naw, screw that. [*He exits.*]

DANIEL: Go ahead and read, and we'll interpret. [*He poses.*]

JESS: Well, okay. [*Reading.*] *Troilus and Cressida* was written in 1603, published in quarto in 1604, and appears in the First Folio, although this version is some one hundred and sixty-six lines longer than the second quarto edition of 1645, which is some one hundred and sixty-six lines shorter.

[*During the above,* DANIEL *and* ADAM *perform a bizarre performance-art interpretation of* JESS's *text involving dance, weird toys, props, a Godzilla robot (or any toy with exquisite comic timing). The performance escalates and becomes so far-out that the audience ceases to listen to* JESS *and are only watching the surreal performance.*]

JESS: Stop it. STOP IT!! You're making a mockery of my scholarship!

DANIEL: Yeah. Adam, lose the Godzilla.

[ADAM *stomps off petulantly, taking props and toys with him.*]

DANIEL: Jess, just spitballing, but— [*Indicating the monograph.*] Is there something in there about the plot?

[ADAM *re-enters with a crown.*]

JESS: Plot? Of course I cover the plot. Right here in the footnote on page ninety-seven. [*Reading.*] 'Troilus, youngest son of Priam, King of Troy—'

ADAM: Okay, you be Troilus and you [*Crowning* JESS.] be the King.

JESS: Okay, great. [*Reading.*] '—loves Cressida . . .'

[JESS *and* DANIEL *look at* ADAM.]

ADAM: I'll get the wig. [ADAM *exits, fetches the wig and re-enters.*]

JESS: '. . . and has arranged with her uncle Pandarus for a meeting. Although she feigns indifference, she is attracted to him.'

ADAM: I have to feign indifference?!

JESS: [*To* ADAM.] Yes. [*Reading.*] 'Meanwhile, Agamemnon, the Greek commander—'

ADAM AND DANIEL: *Agamemnon*?!

ADAM: Bo-ring!

DANIEL: Sorry, Jess, you know I love your brain, but all this footnotey Greek stuff is too much.

ADAM: Yeah, like as soon as you said 'Agamemnon,' I was asleep. No, I'm sorry, but I promised myself I would not do dry, boring, vomitless Shakespeare for these people. [*Indicating the audience.*] Because it'll just turn them off to it. Like, when I was in school and we were supposed to be studying Shakespeare, I'd be looking out the window at the kids playing ball, and thinking, 'Why can't this Shakespeare stuff be more like sports?!'

JESS: Sports?

DANIEL: How do you mean?

ADAM: Well, sports are exciting. Engaging. I mean, take the histories, for example. With all those kings and queens knocking each other off, running up and down the field, the throne passing from one to the next—it's exactly like playing football, but you do it with a crown.

DANIEL: Hey, they are kinda similar, aren't they?

JESS: Yeah, I can see that! Line 'em up!

[*They snap into a three-man football formation:* ADAM *at center,* DANIEL *at quarter-back,* JESS *at nose tackle.*]

DANIEL: [*Barking out signals.*] Green nineteen! Omaha! Pontefract! Richard III! Henry IV, Part One, Part Two—

ALL: HUP!

J/ANNOUNCER: The crown is snapped to Richard the Second, that well-spoken fourteenth-century monarch. He's fading back to pass, looking for an heir downfield, but there's a heavy rush from King John. [*J/KING JOHN stabs D/ RICHARD II.*]

D/RICHARD II: "My gross flesh sinks downwards!"

[*J/KING JOHN dies, tossing the crown in the air. A/HENRY VI picks it up.*]

J/ANNOUNCER: The crown is in the air, and Henry the Sixth comes up with it!

A/HENRY VI: Victory is mine!

[*J/KING JOHN knocks down A/HENRY VI.*]

D/ANNOUNCER: But he's hit immediately by King John. Oh no! He's cutting Henry the Sixth into three parts. That's gotta hurt!

[*J/KING JOHN mimes slicing up A/HENRY VI.*]

This could be the end of the War of the Roses cycle!

[*J/KING JOHN grabs the crown and runs with it.*]

A/ANNOUNCER: King John is in the clear . . .

J/KING JOHN: "My soul hath elbow room!"

A/ANNOUNCER: He's at the forty, the thirty, the twenty—

[DANIEL *sneaks up from behind and mimes pouring something into* J/KING JOHN's *mouth.*]

Ooh, but he's *poisoned* on the ten-yard line!

[DANIEL *snatches the crown and puts it on, becoming* KING LEAR. JESS *exits.*]

Looks like he's out for the game. Replacing him now is number seventy-two, King Lear.

D/LEAR: [*Draws a play on his hand.*] To Regan and Goneril I'll hand off my kingdom. Cordelia, you go long.

[JESS *enters as a* REFEREE, *throwing a penalty flag and blowing a whistle.*]

A/ANNOUNCER: There's a penalty marker!

[J/REFEREE *makes a hand signal and points at* D/LEAR.]

Fictional character on the field. Lear is disqualified, and he's not happy about it.

D/LEAR: [*Handing over the crown.*] Wankers!

A/ANNOUNCER: [*Takes the crown, plays center.*] Lining up now is that father-son team of Henry the Fourth and Prince Hal. Center snaps to the quarterback. Quarterback gives to the hunchback.

[*The crown is passed from* J/HENRY IV *to* A/HENRY V *to* D/RICHARD III, *who limps across the stage like a crowned Quasimodo.*]

It looks like Richard the Third's limp is giving him trouble!

D/RICHARD III: "A horse, a horse! My kingdom for a horse!"

[JESS *tackles* D/RICHARD III. *A dummy comes flying from the wings, adding to the pile.*]

A/ANNOUNCER: There's a pile-up on the field.

[*The crown rolls away and is scooped up by* A/HENRY VIII. *He runs.*]

D/ANNOUNCER: *Fum-ble!* And Henry the Eighth comes up with it. He's at the fifteen. The ten. He stops at the five-yard-line to chop off his wife's head—

A/HENRY VIII: [*Mimes decapitating Anne Boleyn.*] Huzzah!

D/ANNOUNCER: *Touchdown* for the Red Rose! Oh, my! You gotta believe this is the beginning of a Tudor Dynasty!

ALL/CHEERLEADERS: Henry the Fifth! Richard the Third! The whole royal family's frickin' absurd! Go, Megan!!

[DANIEL *and* JESS *congratulate each other as* ADAM *clambers into the audience.*]

ADAM: Can I have some house lights please? [*To an audience member.*] Can I borrow your program for a sec? [He *grabs a program from a patron, which must contain a* LIST OF SHAKESPEARE'S PLAYS.]

DANIEL: What are you doing?

[ADAM *flips through the program and opens it to the list of plays, displaying it so that* JESS *and* DANIEL *can see.*]

ADAM: I just want to check the list of plays. I think we might have done 'em all already.

JESS: Really?

[*They all lean in to consult the program.*]

ADAM: Yeah, see, we did all the histories just now—

DANIEL: The comedies were 'a lump of hilarity.'

JESS: Okay, that leaves the tragedies. We did *Titus Andronicus* with all the blood—

[JESS *and* DANIEL *start pointing out plays in the program.*]

ADAM: *Romeo and Juliet* we did—

DANIEL: *Julius Caesar, Troilus and Cressida*, check and check—

ADAM: I did *Othello* with boats.

JESS: [*To* ADAM.] Don't remind me! [*Back to the program.*] Lear was in the football game, *Macbeth* we did with Scottish accents.

DANIEL: What about *Antony and Cleopatra*?

ADAM: Yeah, I threw up on someone over there.

DANIEL: Right. [*To the person he threw up on.*] Hope you enjoyed 'Throw Up Thursday!'

JESS: *Timon of Athens* and *Coriolanus* had cameos in the baking show.

ADAM: And that's it, right? That's all of them! [*Points to the program.*] Comedies, histories, tragedies—Boom!

DANIEL: Wow. Great. [*To audience.*] Looks like we can let you go a little early.

JESS: Hey, no, look . . . [*Points to a spot in the program.*]

ALL: Oh, no . . . *Hamlet!*

ADAM: Shakespeare didn't write *Hamlet.*

DANIEL: Sure he did.

JESS: You know, the young prince struggling with his conscience after his uncle murders his father?

ADAM: Um . . . That's *The Lion King.*

JESS: [*To audience.*] This is it, my friends. thirty-six plays down, one to go. Perhaps the greatest play ever written. A play of such lofty poetic and philosophical—

ADAM: [*Tugging at* JESS's *sleeve.*] Wait a minute, Jess. *Hamlet* is a serious, hard-core play, and I'm just not up for it right now.

JESS: Whaddaya mean? It's the last one!

ADAM: I know. It's just that that football game left me emotionally and physically drained. I don't think I could do it justice.

DANIEL: We don't have to do it justice. We just have to do it.

JESS: We can do this, Adam. I know *Hamlet* backward and forward.

ADAM: Well, I don't know it backward, and I don't wanna do it!

JESS: But the show's called *The Complete Works of William Shakespeare.*

ADAM: *Abridged!* I'm abridging.

DANIEL: Adam, I think the audience really wants to see it. [*To audience.*] What do you say, would you like to see *Hamlet*? [*Audience responds.*]

ADAM: Okay, fine. We'll do *Hamlet*.

DANIEL and JESS: Great—

ADAM: As a two-person show! If you feel so strongly about it, then YOU do it. I'm outta here!

[ADAM *jumps off the stage.*]

DANIEL: Hey, where do you think you're going?

JESS: Get back here!

[JESS *jumps into the audience and tries to pull him back; they struggle.*]

ADAM: No, no, NO! [*Then as if changing his mind.*] Okay, okay, OKAY! Just don't touch me!

[JESS *lets go.* ADAM *starts to run.*]

DANIEL: We've got a runner! Somebody stop him!

[ADAM *grabs a young audience member.*]

ADAM: I'll kill this kid! I'll kill him!

DANIEL: Fine, but that'll definitely turn him off to Shakespeare.

[ADAM *lets go of his hostage and runs out the back of the house.*]

JESS: I'm gonna kill YOU, you Shakespeare snowflake!

[JESS *follows, slamming the door behind him. We hear* ADAM *scream once in the lobby. Then silence. They are gone.* DANIEL *returns to the stage alone.*]

DANIEL: [*After a looong beat.*] Don't worry, Jess is usually much faster than Adam.

[*He sighs in frustration. He gets an idea and brightens up. He consults the book, flipping through a few pages. He runs offstage, and re-enters a moment later dressed as a guard and carrying a sword.*]

D/BERNARDO: "Who's there?

D/HORATIO: [*Using another voice and changing his posture.*] Nay, answer me. Stand and unfold yourself.

D/BERNARDO: Long live the King.

D/HORATIO: Bernardo?"

[DANIEL *realizes how lame this is, and stops.*]

DANIEL: So, a horse walks into a bar. And the bartender says . . . [*He's got nothing.*] F*ck. [*NOTE: the horse joke is just the briefest possible stall here. The actor may choose to tell another joke or two, play a short tune on a musical instrument, maybe do an impression or a party trick. Then:*] So, I had this weird dream the other night. Typical actor's nightmare. We were doing THIS show, and it's going great, we're making really good time, but then I realize that we haven't actually read all the plays, and we're just making stuff up as we go along. Then Adam and Jess just disappear, and I'm left totally alone on the stage with an hour to fill. And there's this vague, sinister threat waiting in the wings. And then suddenly the lights go out and it's intermission. And I'm naked.

[*As* DANIEL *drops his trousers . . . BLACKOUT.*]

[*Lights come up in the house.* DANIEL *is gone.*]

<u>INTERMISSION</u>

Act Two

LIGHTS UP. *After a beat*, DANIEL *enters costumed as* HORATIO, *nervously carrying a spear.*

DANIEL: [*To audience.*] Hi. [*He waits for a response, then:*] Did you have a nice intermission? [*He again waits for a response.*] Yeah? What'd you do? [*He waits for a response.*] Nice. Was there a long line at the ladies' room? [*Of course there was.*] Yeah, I hate that. [*Awkward pause, then:*] So Jess and Adam aren't back yet. I— [*A cell phone rings.*] Okay, who didn't turn off their phone!? You are in so much trouble! [*Rings again.*] Oh crap, it's mine. [*He pulls out a phone, looks at it. To audience:*] It's Jess! [*He answers it. To phone.*] Jess, where are you!? . . . Oh. Which airport? . . . Do you have Adam? . . . [*He breathes a sigh of relief and gives the audience a thumbs-up. Then, worried:*] Well, what am I supposed to do in the meantime? Oh. Okay. Good. Okay, bye. Wait, don't give Adam any candy, you know his blood sugar . . . [*But* JESS *has already hung up.*] Jess? [*Ends call.*]

Okay, they're on their way back, they'll be here any minute. While we're waiting, Jess reminded me that I should cover the sonnets. [*He pulls out a single index card.*] Ahem. Shakespeare wrote one hundred and fifty-four Shakespearean sonnets. We've condensed them onto this three-by-five card, and I was thinking maybe what we could do is pass it among the audience. Like if we start right here with you [*Indicating a member of the audience.*], you take it, read it, enjoy it, then pass it to the person next to you and so on down the row, and then you pass it behind you, and so on, back and forth and back and forth and back and then if *you* wouldn't mind running it up to the balcony? Thanks, and then . . . forth and back and forth and back, and by the time it gets to *you* [*At the end of the last row.*] . . . Jess and Adam should be back.

So Bob, if we could have some house lights please? Ready? Okay, here we go: Shakespeare's sonnets! [*Hands the card to the first person in the front row of the audience.*] That first one's really good. [*Begins to hum a 'waiting tune' on a kazoo.*]

[JESS *and* ADAM *enter at the back of the house and approach the stage.*]

ADAM: Hi honey, we're home!

DANIEL: Jess and Adam, everybody! [*Retrieves the sonnet card.*]

ADAM: [*Excited.*] We're back and ready to do *Hamlet!* Woo-hoo! [*To audience:*] Give me an H-E-L! [*Audience responds.*] Give me an M-E-T! [*Audience responds.*] What's that spell?

DANIEL and JESS and AUDIENCE: 'Helmet.'

ADAM: Yeah! I gotta go put on my *helmet!* Woo-hoo! H-E-L . . . [*Exits.*]

DANIEL: You gave him sugar, didn't you?

JESS: No, I told him if he did *Hamlet* I'd take him to see [*Insert name of current Broadway show that audiences love but critics hate.*]

DANIEL: *Again?* Oy.

[DANIEL *exits.*]

JESS: Right, where were we? Thirty-six plays down, one to go. Bob, could you please set the scene for perhaps the greatest play ever written in the English language? [*The lights change back to the moody night scene. Melodramatically.*] 'Helmet, the Tra— . . . *Hamlet,* the Tragedy . . . of the Prince . . . of Denmark.' The place: [*Well, duh.*] . . . Denmark. The battlements of Elsinore castle. Midnight. Two guards enter.

[JESS *exits. Enter* ADAM *as* BERNARDO *and* DANIEL *as* HORATIO, *opposite.*]

A/BERNARDO: "Who's there?

D/HORATIO: Nay, answer me. Stand and unfold yourself.

A/BERNARDO: Long live the King.

D/HORATIO: Bernardo?

A/BERNARDO: He. 'Tis now struck twelve. Get thee to bed, Fellatio.

D/HORATIO: [*Correcting him.*] Horatio! For this relief, much thanks.

A/BERNARDO: Well, good night.

D/HORATIO: Peace, break thee off. Look where it comes!

[*The 'Ghost of Hamlet's Father' enters. Okay, it's just a sweat sock with a happy face drawn on it with a Sharpie, dangling from a fishing line upstage center.*]

JESS: [*Offstage ghostly moaning sounds.*]

A/BERNARDO: Mark it, Horatio. It would be spoke to.

D/HORATIO: What art thou? By heaven, I charge thee, speak!

JESS: [*Sound of a cock crowing.*]

[*The sock is yanked offstage.*]

D/HORATIO: 'Tis gone!

A/BERNARDO: It was about to speak when the crew sock—sock cr—*cock crew.*

D/HORATIO: Break we our watch up; and by my advice, let us impart what we have seen tonight unto—

BOTH: Hamlet, Prince of Denmark!

[*They exit together. Lights change to day.* JESS *enters as* HAMLET.]

J/HAMLET: O that this too too solid flesh would melt,
Thaw, and resolve itself into a dew.
That it should come to this, but two months dead.
So loving to my mother. [*Points to a woman in the audience.*]
Frailty, thy name is woman!" [*Beat.*] Yeah, you!!
"Married with mine uncle, my father's brother.
Thy funeral baked meats did coldly furnish forth
The marriage tables.

[D/HORATIO *and* A/BERNARDO *appear in the upstage left doorway, observing* J/HAMLET's *fit of melancholy.* A/BERNARDO *nods for* D/HORATIO *to approach him.* D/HORATIO *enters as* A/BERNARDO *disappears.*]

D/HORATIO: My lord!

J/HAMLET: Horatio!

[They exchange an elaborate Wittenberg University Danish Club handshake. Then:]

Methinks I see my father.

D/HORATIO: Where, my lord?

J/HAMLET: In my mind's eye, Horatio.

D/HORATIO: My lord, I think I saw him yesternight.

J/HAMLET: Saw who?

D/HORATIO: The king, your father.

J/HAMLET: The king my father? But where was this?

D/HORATIO: Upon the platform where we watched.

J/HAMLET: 'Tis very strange. I will watch tonight.
Perchance 'twill walk again. All is not well.
Would the night were come.

[The lighting changes abruptly from day to night. JESS and DANIEL are impressed. They give a thumbs-up to the light booth and commence pretending to be cold.]

J/HAMLET: The air bites shrewdly. It is very cold.

D/HORATIO: Look, my lord, it comes!

J/HAMLET: Angels and ministers of grace defend us.
Something is rotten in the state of Denmark.

[ADAM enters as the GHOST OF HAMLET'S FATHER. Beneath his armor he wears a ghostly robe that resembles a giant sweat sock.]

A/GHOST: Mark me!

J/HAMLET: Speak. I am bound to hear.

A/GHOST: So art thou to revenge when thou shalt hear.
If ever thou didst thy dear father love
Revenge his foul and most unnatural murther.

J/HAMLET: Murther!

D/HORATIO: Murther!

A/GHOST: The serpent that did sting thy father's life
Now wears his crown.

J/HAMLET: My uncle!

D/HORATIO: Your uncle!

A/GHOST: Let not the royal bed of Denmark
Become a couch for incest."

J/HAMLET: Incest!

D/HORATIO: A couch!

A/GHOST: "Adieu, Hamlet, remember me! [*Exits.*]

D/HORATIO: My lord, this is strange.

J/HAMLET: There are more things in heaven and earth
Than are dreamt of in your philosophy."
So PISS OFF! [*Slaps him.*]

[D/HORATIO *exits.*]

"I hereafter shall think meat . . ."

[*A quick reverie.*]

Mmm, bacon . . .

[*Back in character.*]

"To put an antic disposition on.
The time is out of joint.
O cursed spite that ever I was born to exit right!

[J/HAMLET *exits left, then, embarrassed, re-enters and exits right. Lights change to day.* DANIEL *enters as* POLONIUS. *He takes his time, totters slowly downstage center, wheezing, until finally . . .*]

D/POLONIUS: Neither a borrower nor a lender be.

[*He is tremendously satisfied with himself. He waddles toward the upstage right door where he is run over by* ADAM, *entering screaming as* OPHELIA.]

A/OPHELIA: Aaaaaaaaaaaaaaaaaa!

D/POLONIUS: How now, Ophelia. What's the matter?

A/OPHELIA: My lord, as I was sewing in my closet,
Lord Hamlet, with his doublet all unbraced,
No hat upon his head, pale as his shirt,
His knees knocking each other, and with a look
So piteous in purport as if he had been loosed
Out of hell to speak of horrors, he comes before me.

D/POLONIUS: Mad for thy love?

A/OPHELIA: Aaaaaaaaaaa! I know not.

D/POLONIUS: Why, this is the very ecstasy of love.
I have found the cause of Hamlet's lunacy.
Since brevity is the soul of wit, I will be brief:
He is mad.

[J/HAMLET *enters reading a book, feigning madness.*]

Look you where the poor wretch comes reading.
Away, I do beseech you.

[A/OPHELIA *exits.*]

How does my good lord Hamlet?

J/HAMLET: Well, God-a-mercy.

D/POLONIUS: Do you know me, my lord?

J/HAMLET: Excellent well. You are a fishmonger.

D/POLONIUS: What do you read, my lord?

J/HAMLET: Words, words, words.

D/POLONIUS: [*Aside.*] Though this be madness, yet there's method in't."

[A/OPHELIA *pokes her head out from backstage.*]

A/OPHELIA: [*Fast.*] Daddy, the Players are here and they say they want to do a play-within-a-play whatever that means. [*Beat.*] That's all.

[A/OPHELIA *disappears.*]

D/POLONIUS: [*Bowing.*] My lord.

[D/POLONIUS *follows* A/OPHELIA *off.*]

J/HAMLET: "I am but mad north-northwest.
  I'll have these players play something like
  The murther of my father before mine uncle.
  I'll observe his looks. If he do but blench,
  I know my course. The play's the thing
  Wherein I'll catch the conscience of the king!

[J/HAMLET *kneels and draws a dagger. Lights blackout to a pin-spot, which misses* JESS *by several feet; he has to slide over to it, while trying to maintain his serious composure.* JESS *gets into a 'method' space for his speech. He's into it. Maybe too far into it . . .*]

  To be, or not to be? That is the question.
  Whether 'tis nobler in the mind to suffer
  The slings and arrows of outrageous fortune
  Or to take arms against a sea of troubles
  And by opposing end them. [*He's definitely too intense now.*]
  To die; to sleep;"
  To sleep . . . perchance to nap . . . [JESS *has gone to a very dark place. With rising panic.*] To . . . nap . . . my nappy time. In my crib and mommy's gone and my head is stuck in the rails and there's a clown! A scary clown puppet!! And it's laughing! Laughing at ME!!!

[JESS *screams and collapses, sobbing, into a nervous breakdown.* DANIEL *and* ADAM *rush in to comfort him.*]

ADAM: Bob, lights please! [*Stage lights come up.*]

DANIEL: Jess, get a grip!

ADAM: What happened to your speech?

JESS: I was so into it. I mean, way deep in the method, really feeling Hamlet's fear in the face of oblivion. But . . . then suddenly there was a clown's face. Laughing at me. They ALL laugh at me. Just like they laugh at Teresa. [*Sobs.*]

ADAM: Teresa?

DANIEL: Is that his girlfriend?

ADAM: I have no idea.

JESS: Oh my god, do you two *not* watch *Real Housewives of New Jersey*?! Teresa tries so hard to be good, but she went to jail, and then her husband went to jail, and then her mom died and then her dad had a heart attack and he finally died and Melissa has *never* been supportive. [*Of course this bit changes weekly or monthly, as* JESS *updates the audience on the trauma of the latest Housewife drama, or whatever incredibly schlocky show you care to comment on.*] And you don't even care! [*Collapses into more sobs.*]

ADAM: [*Stunned.*] You watch *Real Housewives*?

JESS: [*Defensive at first, then the floodgates open.*] I watched one episode as research for an updated *Merry Wives of Windsor* but then I just couldn't stop. *Total Divas, Hillbilly Wife Swap, Bachelorette* . . . all of 'em.

DANIEL: So, wait a minute. All that stuff you were spouting about killing our televisions and embracing the Bard—that was all B.S.?

JESS: [*Feebly.*] No.

ADAM: Jess, you're not really a preeminent Shakespeare scholar at all, are you?

JESS: [*Mumbles something.*]

ADAM: ARE YOU!?

JESS: [*Blurting out his big confession.*] I'm not even post-eminent!!

DANIEL: But—you took that course.

JESS: I didn't finish it.

DANIEL: I saw your certificate!

JESS: I made it in Photoshop.

DANIEL: I . . . I don't even know who you are!

JESS: I thought the world of Shakespearean scholarship would be all fast cars and hot babes. But it's not! It's all folios and quatrains and ibids . . . So cold. But when I'm in Jersey, everyone's so young and bold and beautiful and restless, and I tried to bring that to Shakespeare, but then . . . they just laugh at me.

[JESS *collapses in a heap, sobbing.*]

ADAM: [*To* DANIEL.] He's toast. [*To audience.*] Sorry, folks, we're gonna have to skip the whole monologue.

DANIEL: We can't skip 'To be or not to be,' it's the most famous soliloquy in all of Shakespeare.

ADAM: It's overrated.

DANIEL: Overrated!?

ADAM: Think about it. Hamlet is supposed to be killing his uncle and suddenly he's talking about killing himself. Where did *that* come from? It completely weakens his character.

DANIEL: It makes it more complex. The layers give it meaning.

ADAM: No, the layers make it suck. It's just too many words—like that one speech that goes: "I have of late, but wherefore I know not, lost all my mirth, forgone all custom of exercise; and indeed it goes so heavily with my disposition that this goodly frame, the earth, seems to me a sterile promontory; this most excellent canopy, the air, look you; this brave o'erhanging firmament, this majestical roof fretted with golden fire, why it appeareth no other thing to me than a foul and pestilent congregation of vapors. What a piece of work is a man; how noble in reason, how infinite in faculty, in form and moving how express and admirable; in action how like an angel; in apprehension how like a god. The beauty of the world, the paragon of animals; and yet to me, what is this quintessence of dust? Man delights not me." [*He has delivered the speech simply, quietly and without a trace of 'interpretation.' You can hear a pin drop. To* DANIEL.] Okay. That didn't suck.

JESS: [*Still emotional, like a drunk.*] That was beautiful!

[JESS *and* ADAM *share a big, drunken hug.*]

ADAM: I love you!

DANIEL: There, you see? That speech is emotional *and* intellectual. The two can live side-by-side.

JESS: Like Teresa and Melissa?

DANIEL: Um, sure.

ADAM: So when I play Ophelia, I should add some layers?

DANIEL: That would be appreciated. She's not all screams and vomit, you know. There's something going on under that wig.

ADAM: Oh, I get it. Ophelia's complicated. I bet in the 'Get thee to a nunnery' scene, she's probably thinking stuff, and feeling stuff, like, at the same time!

JESS: Exactly.

DANIEL: Yes! Let's do that scene real quick.

JESS: Okay. [*Becoming* HAMLET. *To* ADAM.] "Get thee to a nunnery!"

[*Points at* ADAM. ADAM *stares back blankly.*]

ADAM: What?

JESS: I'm Hamlet, right? [ADAM *nods.*] "Get thee to a nunnery!" [*Beat.*] What does Ophelia reply?

ADAM: [*Flat:*] Aaaa!

JESS: No—with *layers*.

ADAM: [*Nearly the same as before.*] Aaaa!

[DANIEL *and* JESS *shake their heads disapprovingly.*]

DANIEL: No, no, no.

ADAM: Okay, tell me what I'm missing.

JESS: A basic intellectual understanding of the interplay of Ophelia's Id, Ego, and Superego.

ADAM: Okay, anything else?

DANIEL: And an emotional understanding of Ophelia as an oppressed woman.

ADAM: Okay, I need help with this. [*To an individual he takes for a woman in the front row.*] Excuse me . . . do you identify as female?

DANIEL: Adam! Boundaries!

ADAM: Hey, I don't make assumptions. [*To woman.*] What are your preferred pronouns? [*She responds. The performers must use the person's pronoun choice for the rest of the bit. The following assumes 'she/her.'*] Thanks, this will only take a minute. [ADAM *leads her to the stage.*]

DANIEL: I don't think it's a good idea to bring a total stranger onstage.

ADAM: She's not strange. She's just . . . [*Assesses her.*] a 'free spirit.' [*To* VOLUNTEER.] Okay, what's your name? [*She responds.*] Do you mind if we call you 'Bob?' It's a little easier to remember. Okay, Bob, we need you to help us go really deep into Ophelia's brain and do a . . . um . . . what would you call it?

JESS: A Freudian analysis.

ADAM: Exactly! A Floridian analysis.

JESS: It's very simple: Hamlet is playing out sublimated childhood neuroses, displacing repressed Oedipal desires into sexualized anger toward Ophelia—

DANIEL: Hamlet's being a prick.

JESS: Hello, I just said that.

ADAM: So Hamlet gets all worked up and tells Ophelia to get out of his life. He says, "Get thee to a nunnery." And in response, Ophelia screams.

JESS: Hamlet says, "Get thee to a nunnery," and Ophelia screams. Let's give it a try. "Get thee to a nunnery!"

[*The* VOLUNTEER *screams, probably not very well.*]

ADAM: Did you hear that, Daniel? I thought that was great.

JESS: [*Unsure.*] Yeah, it was okay.

DANIEL: No, it kinda sucked. Look, we might as well be honest. There's no point just humoring her.

ADAM: Come on, give her a break. I mean, okay, she's not an actor—and frankly it shows. [*To* VOLUNTEER.] But I think you showed a lot of heart. A lot of courage. A lot of, as Shakespeare would say, *chutzpah*. And to get a better scream, I think we just need get everybody involved in this. You know, create a supportive environment for Bob here. [*Indicating the* VOLUNTEER.]

JESS: We could divide the audience up into Ophelia's Id, Ego, and Superego!

DANIEL: Cool, I'll get an Ego. Bob, bring up the house lights, please?

[*The house lights come up.* DANIEL *grabs someone out of the audience and hustles them up onstage.*]

JESS: Now, you're playing the part of Ophelia's Ego. At this point in the play, her Ego is feeling assaulted, it's in flight mode—it's an Ego on the run.

DANIEL: Why don't we symbolize this by—wait, name and pronouns? [EGO *responds.*] Cool, but do you mind if we call you 'Bob?' Okay, so we'll symbolize this by actually having you run back and forth across the stage in front of Ophelia. Will you give that a try? Right now, just—

ALL: Go, go, go, go, go, go!

[EGO *runs from one side of the stage to the other, but is stopped before beginning a second round trip.*]

DANIEL: Wow! An ego *maniac!*

ADAM: Bob is not a maniac, Bob is a 'free spirit.' [*To audience.*] Now, everyone in the front two rows, why don't you be Ophelia's Id. That's like the watery depths of Ophelia's soul, right, Jess?

JESS: [*Shrugs reluctant agreement.*] Sure, why not.

ADAM: And she's tossed by the tides and the currents of her emotions. So everybody in the first two rows, hands in the air, wave them back and forth, kind of undulate, and say, [*Falsetto.*] 'Maybe . . . maybe not . . . maybe . . . maybe not.'

[*Following* ADAM's *lead, the front rows raise their hands in the air and gently undulate them from side to side chanting 'Maybe . . . maybe not . . . maybe . . . maybe not . . .'*]

JESS: Beautiful! Now why don't we get everybody behind the first two rows to be Ophelia's Superego. The Superego is that jumble of voices inside your head that dominate your moral and ethical behavior. It's very powerful, very difficult to shake . . . some people never shake it in their entire lifetime.

ADAM: Sorta like Catholicism.

JESS: Exactly.

ADAM: So let's divide the Superego into three parts. Everybody from where Jess is indicating—

[JESS, *indicating with his dagger, slices off the left half of the orchestra seats.*]

—to my left will be Section 'A.' Everybody in this half of the orchestra, you're Section 'B.' And everybody up in the cheap seats, you're section . . .? [*He prompts the audience to respond. They call out, 'C.'*]

ADAM: Yeah. Not too bloody difficult.

JESS: Let's make Section A that part of Ophelia's brain that's bought into the dominant paradigm and considers herself worthless unless proven otherwise.

ADAM: Right! So she's telling herself, 'Who are you kidding?! You're just a complete waste of space!' . . . [*To* VOLUNTEER.] No offense, Bob. [*To audience.*] We'll use Hamlet's line for this—you all say, "Get thee to a nunnery!" Let's try it. Section A?

[ADAM *signals Section A like a conductor. Section A shouts "Get thee to a nunnery!"*]

DANIEL: Section A, that was awful.

ADAM: C'mon, people, work with us on this. We want it very loud, very strident. Section A?

[*Section A responds more forcefully.*]

JESS: Yes! Much less totally pathetic!

ADAM: Now, I want Section B to represent that part of Ophelia's psyche that wants to go for it.

JESS: Go for it?

ADAM: Yeah, you know—go for it! [*Crudely mimes 'going for it.'*] Huh! Yeah! Netflix and chill!

JESS: Freud would call that the 'libido.'

ADAM: Whatever. [*To audience, Section B.*] Section B, you're saying to Ophelia, 'Go for it, girl! Put on that spendy makeup, jerk Hamlet's jerkin, and saddle up your nasty nun on his baloney pony!'

JESS: There's nothing in the Shakespearean text about a 'baloney pony', but there is a good reference to makeup. Why don't we have them say, "Paint an inch thick!"

ADAM: Perfect! Give it a try. Section B? [*They respond with "Paint an inch thick."*]

DANIEL: Section A, you could learn something from Section B.

ADAM: Now Section C, you're the most important layer of them all. We're going to use you to make Ophelia relevant to women of the twenty-first century.

JESS: She refuses to be window-dressing in the oppressive, male-primogenitive power structure of the Danish court.

DANIEL: Right. She's like the CEO of a floral delivery start-up. She doesn't need Hamlet's little dramas dragging her down.

ADAM: Exactly! She's a sister doing it to herself and she's telling Hamlet, 'Screw you, screw Polonius, and screw the Danish patriarchy!'

DANIEL: [*To ADAM, sotto voce.*] Whoa. Adam. That was beautiful. Why don't we just have them say those exact words?

ADAM: [*Sotto.*] Seriously?

JESS: [*Sotto.*] It's perfect.

ADAM: [*To audience, section C.*] Okay, yeah. Section C, you're gonna tell Hamlet . . .

ALL: 'Screw you, screw Polonius, and screw the Danish patriarchy!'

ADAM: Let's give it a try, shall we? Section C?

[*Section C responds by loudly shouting "Screw you, screw Polonius, and screw the Danish patriarchy!"*]

DANIEL: I thought that was a fantastic C-section.

ADAM: Totally! [*To the* VOLUNTEER.] So now, Bob. We're going to get all of this Floridian stuff going at once: the Ego, the Superego—

JESS: The Id, 'Maybe, maybe not—'

DANIEL: Your feminist rage is boiling over—

ADAM: Now your job as an actress is to take all of these voices and blend them deep within your soul. We're going to whip everyone into a mighty frenzy, then stop everything, all attention goes to you, and you let out with that earth-shattering scream that epitomizes Ophelia. [*Beat.*] Ah, she can't wait.

DANIEL: Okay everybody, let's all take a deep breath. [*They do. To a random audience member.*] Let it out.

ADAM: [*To* VOLUNTEER OPHELIA.] And remember, no matter what happens—

ALL: Act natural.

ADAM: Okay, start with the Ego.

DANIEL: Ready, Bob, on your mark, get set, go!

[*The* EGO *runs back and forth across the stage.*]

JESS: Id, arms up. 'Maybe, maybe not . . .'

ADAM: [*Building to mighty frenzy:*] Section A . . . Section B . . . Section C . . . A . . . B . . . C . . . A . . . ABABCBA . . .

[*Audience responds:* EGO *on stage is running back and forth. The front rows are undulating their arms in the air intoning, 'Maybe, maybe not . . . .' Half the orchestra is repeatedly shouting 'Get thee to a nunnery!' The other half of the orchestra is repeatedly shouting 'Paint an inch thick!' The balconies are yelling, 'Screw you, screw Polonius, and screw the Danish patriarchy!' over and over.* ADAM, JESS *and* DANIEL *are acting as conductors, signaling the different sections, building the tempo, and whipping everyone into a frenzy. Finally,* ADAM *signals that everyone should stop.*]

ADAM: Okay, STOP!

[*The chaos stops abruptly.* ADAM, JESS, *and* DANIEL *gesture dramatically toward the* VOLUNTEER *indicating that she should scream. She is hit with a DRAMATIC RED SPOTLIGHT.*]

VOLUNTEER: Aaaaaaaaaaaaaaaaaaa!

[*The audience goes wild.* ALL *thank her.* ADAM *and* JESS *exit as* DANIEL *walks volunteers back to their seats.*]

DANIEL: Let's hear it for Bob. And Bob! [*Shouting to the lighting booth.*] House lights out, Bob? [*The house lights fade out as* DANIEL *returns to the stage.*] Boy, we really shared something there, didn't we? But we digress. Back to *Hamlet*, act three, scene two: the pivotal play-within-a-play scene, in which Hamlet discovers conclusive evidence that his uncle murthered his father.

[DANIEL *exits.* J/HAMLET *enters, pauses, then whips his hands out from behind his back to reveal sock-puppet 'Players' on his hands.*]

J/HAMLET: "Speak the speech, I pray you, as I pronounced it to you, trippingly on the tongue. Suit the action to the word, the word to the action, and hold, as 'twere, the mirror up to nature. [D/POLONIUS *enters with a puppet theater.*] Will my lord hear this piece of work?

D/POLONIUS: Aye, and the king, too, presently.

[*Trumpet fanfare.* ADAM *enters as* CLAUDIUS, *an evil king wearing a crown and an ugly beard.*]

A/CLAUDIUS: And now, how does my cousin Hamlet, and my son?

J/HAMLET: A little more than kin, and less than kind.

A/CLAUDIUS: I have nothing with this answer Hamlet, these words are not mine."

D/POLONIUS: Take a seat, my lord.

A/CLAUDIUS: [*Moves into audience.*] Very well. [*He aggressively takes his same seat from the show's opening, addressing the adjacent theater-goer.*] What are you looking at, libtard?

[J/HAMLET *ducks behind the puppet theater.*]

D/POLONIUS: My lord, the Royal Theater of Denmark is proud to present *The Murther of Gonzago.*

A/CLAUDIUS: A puppet show! [*Yelling to the rafters.*] Hey, Adult Puppet Show Guy, drink liberal tears!

D/POLONIUS: My lord, act one.

[J/HAMLET *performs a romantic puppet dumbshow: the King puppet and Queen puppet meeting, falling in love, and promptly humping.* D/POLONIUS *breaks in.*]

Intermission!

J/HAMLET: How likes my lord the play?

A/CLAUDIUS: The lady doth protest too much, methinks!" [*Laughs uproariously. To the person adjacent.*] She was asking for it, right? [*To rest of audience.*] C'mon, you all know she wanted it!

D/POLONIUS: [*Chiding.*] My lord, are we forgetting a certain women's movement?

A/CLAUDIUS: Oh, MeToo, boo-hoo!

D/POLONIUS: My lord, act two.

A/CLAUDIUS: Gesundheit. Har har! I'm on fire!

[*The puppet King lies down to sleep. A puppet shark dressed like Claudius appears and attacks the King!* A/CLAUDIUS *rises, storms on stage, rips the puppets off of* J/HAMLET'S *hands.*]

D/POLONIUS: "The king rises.

A/CLAUDIUS: Give o'er the play! Lights! Away!

[*A/CLAUDIUS exits with puppets. D/POLONIUS strikes the puppet theater.*]

J/HAMLET: I'll take the ghost's word for a thousand pound!

D/POLONIUS: My lord, the queen would speak with you in her closet.

J/HAMLET: Then will I come to my mother" who's in the closet. [*Exits.*]

D/POLONIUS: "Behind the arras I'll convey myself to hear the process. [*Hides.*]

[*Enter ADAM as GERTRUDE and J/HAMLET, opposite.*]

J/HAMLET: Now, mother, what's the matter?

A/GERTRUDE: Hamlet, thou hast thy father much offended.

[*J/HAMLET draws his dagger.*]

J/HAMLET: Mother, you have my father much offended.

A/GERTRUDE: What wilt thou do? Thou wilt not murther me? Help! [*Exits.*]

D/POLONIUS: Help! Help!

J/HAMLET: How now? A rat!"

[*J/HAMLET charges at D/POLONIUS with his dagger, then suddenly shifts into slow motion. Lights strobe and we hear the music from the shower scene in* Psycho.]

D/POLONIUS: [*Slo-mo voice.*] Ooooh noooo, thaaaat willllll huuuuurt!

[*J/HAMLET stabs D/POLONIUS in exaggerated slow motion. D/POLONIUS exits as he dies. J/HAMLET licks his dagger clean and then snaps out of slo-mo as the strobe effect ends.*]

J/HAMLET: "Dead for a ducat, dead!

[*A/CLAUDIUS enters.*]

A/CLAUDIUS: Now, Hamlet, where's Polonius?

J/HAMLET: At supper.

A/CLAUDIUS: At supper? Where?

J/HAMLET: Not where he eats, but where he is eaten."

[DANIEL *enters as* LAERTES, *huffing and snarling.*]

A/CLAUDIUS and J/HAMLET: O no, it's Laertes.

A/CLAUDIUS: Son of Polonius.

J/HAMLET: Brother to Ophelia.

A/CLAUDIUS: And a snappy dresser!

D/LAERTES: Why, thanks.
"O thou vile king! Give me my father!
I'll be revenged for Polonius' murther.

JESS: [*Offstage scream imitating* A/OPHELIA.]

[ADAM *realizes he has to change costumes, exits.*]

D/LAERTES: How now, what noise is this?

A/OPHELIA: [*Offstage scream.*]

D/LAERTES: Dear maid, kind sister, sweet Ophelia!

[A/OPHELIA *enters screaming, with flowers.*]

A/OPHELIA: [*Screaming, then singing.*]
They bore him barefaced on the bier
With a hey-nonny-nonny, hey-nonny
And in his grave rained many a tear
With a hey-nonny-nonny ha-cha-cha.
Fare you well my dove."
I'm mad! [*She tosses flowers wildly about.*] I'm out of my tiny little mind! [*To the* VOLUNTEER.] See, this is acting.
"Here's rue for you, and rosemary for remembrance. [*She offers a flower to an audience member.*] And I would have given you violets, but they withered all when my father died"—you *creep!* [*She yanks the flower back.*] I'm starting to feel a little nauseous . . .

[*She lurches into the audience and pretends to vomit on people.*]

D/LAERTES: [*Attempting to carry on despite the chaos* ADAM *is creating in the audience.*] "Hamlet comes back—"

ADAM: [*Leaps back to the stage, super excited.*] Daniel, what's the next scene with Ophelia?

DANIEL: What?

ADAM: What's the next scene with Ophelia?

DANIEL: There are no more scenes with Ophelia. "Hamlet comes back—"

ADAM: But I've got layers now, I'm up for it.

DANIEL: That's all Shakespeare wrote. "Hamlet comes back—"

ADAM: Well, what happens to her?

DANIEL: She drowns.

ADAM: Oh. [*Exits.*]

D/LAERTES: "What would I undertake
To show myself my father's son in deed
More than in words? To—"

[A/OPHELIA *re-enters with a tankard full of water.*]

A/OPHELIA: Here I go.

DANIEL: No, offstage—!

A/OPHELIA: [*She throws the water in her own face.*] Aaaaaaaaa! [*Dies. Stands proudly. Bows. Exits.*]

D/LAERTES: [*Reacts to* ADAM's *hijinks, then, continuing:*]
" . . .To cut his throat in the church.
Aye, and to that end, I'll anoint my sword
With an unction so mortal that where it draws blood
No cataplasm can save the thing from this compulsion."
[*Beat.*] I don't know what it means either.

[D/LAERTES *exits.* J/HAMLET *enters with a skull.*]

J/HAMLET: "This skull had a tongue in it, and could sing once."
And then came—*The Keto Diet.* [*Or insert name of latest fad diet; you know, the one with confirmed deaths.*]
"Alas, poor Yorick! I knew him—
But soft! Here comes the queen.
Couch me awhile, and mark.

[*J/HAMLET leaps into the front row to 'hide.'* A/GERTRUDE *and* D/LAERTES *enter, bearing the corpse of Ophelia—the* DUMMY, *wrapped in a sheet.*]

D/LAERTES: Lay her in the earth; and from her fair
And unpolluted flesh, may violets spring.

J/HAMLET: [*Laughing maniacally, he flings the skull at* ADAM. ADAM *catches it and flings it back, annoyed.*]

A/GERTRUDE: Sweets to the sweet. Farewell.

D/LAERTES: Hold off the earth awhile,
'Til I have caught her once more in mine arms.

J/HAMLET: [*Stands up in the audience.*] What is he whose grief bears such an emphasis? [*He leaps back onto the stage and spikes the skull of Yorick. It's rubber, and bounces away.*] This is I, Hamlet the Great Dane!

[*He rushes to the corpse, and tries to yank it away from* D/LAERTES. *There is a brief tug of war.*]

A/GERTRUDE: Gentlemen! Hamlet! Laertes!

D/LAERTES: The devil take thy soul.

[D/LAERTES *lets go of the corpse as* J/HAMLET *pulls—the corpse catapults backward and smacks* A/GERTRUDE *in the head.* A/GERTRUDE *exits, staggering.*]

J/HAMLET: I will fight with him until my eyelids no longer wag.
The cat will mew, the dog will have his day.
Give us the foils.

D/LAERTES: Come, one for me."

[A/GERTRUDE *runs on and hands a foil to each; then, as she exits:*]

A/GERTRUDE: Now be careful. Those are sharp.

J/HAMLET: "Come, sir.

D/LAERTES: Come, my lord."

[*They fence simply, the pace accelerating.*]

J/HAMLET and D/LAERTES: Clink! Clank! Swish! Poke! Slice! Smack!

[HAMLET *scores a hit.*]

D/LAERTES: Ouch!

J/HAMLET: "One.

D/LAERTES: No!

J/HAMLET: Judgment?

[ADAM *enters. He is ostensibly* CLAUDIUS, *but he hasn't had enough time to make the costume change—he wears parts of three different costumes.*]

A/CLAUDIUS: A hit, a hit; a very palpable hit."

JESS: Who are you supposed to be?

DANIEL: Gertrude!

ADAM: No.

JESS/DANIEL: [*Taking turns rapidly, with* ADAM *replying 'No' to each guess.*] Reynaldo! Osric! Guildenstern! Fortinbras! Voldemort!

A/CLAUDIUS: Close enough! [*Continuing, back in character.*] "Hamlet, here's to thy health. Drink off this cup.

J/HAMLET: Nay, set it by awhile," Uncle . . . Father . . . Mother . . . um, 'They!'

[*They fence.* J/HAMLET *runs* D/LAERTES *completely through.*]

"Another hit. What say you?

D/LAERTES: [*Considers the foil entering his chest and exiting his back.*] A touch. A touch, I do confess.

[A/GERTRUDE *enters with a goblet.*]

A/GERTRUDE: The queen carouses to thy fortune, Hamlet.

D/LAERTES: Madam, do not drink.

A/GERTRUDE: I will, my lord. I pray you pardon me.

D/LAERTES: [*Aside.*] It is the poisoned cup! It is too late.

[A/GERTRUDE *chokes and exits.*]

J/HAMLET: Come, for the third, Laertes."

[*They fence, ultimately running each other through simultaneously.*]

J/HAMLET AND D/LAERTES: Yowch!!

[*Both fall.* A/GERTRUDE *re-enters, staggering from the poisoning and her balloon-breasts noticeably askew.*]

J/HAMLET: "How does the queen?

D/LAERTES: She swoons to see thee bleed.

A/GERTRUDE: No. The drink! The drink! I am poisoned. [*She vomits on the audience until* J/HAMLET *grabs her and spins her offstage.*]

J/HAMLET: O villainy! Treachery! Seek it out!

D/LAERTES: It is here, Hamlet. Here I lie, never to rise again.
I can no more. The king. The king's to blame.

[A/CLAUDIUS *enters, still wearing* GERTRUDE'S *skirt.*]

J/HAMLET: What, the point envenom'd too? Then venom to thy work!
Here, thou incestuous, murth'rous, damned Dane:
Follow my mother!

[J/HAMLET *stabs* A/CLAUDIUS, *who dies.*]

D/LAERTES: Forgive me, Hamlet. I am justly killed by mine own treachery. [*He dies.*]

J/HAMLET: Heaven make thee free of it. I follow thee.
[*To the audience. Seriously.*]
You that look pale, and tremble at this chance
That are but mutes, or audience to this act;
If ever thou didst hold me in thy hearts
Absent thee from felicity awhile;
And in this harsh world draw thy breath in pain
To tell my story. The rest is silence."

[*Dies in a comically dramatic pose.*]

[*Blackout. The lights come back up.* JESS, ADAM, *and* DANIEL *bounce up and bow. Following the applause:*]

JESS: [*To audience.*] You are WELCOME! Thirty-seven plays. Ninety-seven minutes.

DANIEL: Ninety-*five* minutes! We actually finished early.

ADAM: Let's do *Hamlet* again!

DANIEL: In two minutes?

ADAM: We can do it—just cut all the layers.

JESS: Right!

DANIEL: [*To audience.*] My friends, you shall have—

ALL: An encore!

[*While* JESS *and* ADAM *reset the stage and clear props:*]

JESS: [*To audience.*] Folks, we're going to attempt to break the world's record for the fastest performance of *Hamlet*, which is fifty-three seconds. Well, there was a Russian troupe that did it in fifty-one seconds, but they're currently under investigation for doping.

DANIEL: Cool. [*Indicating the wings.*] Puppet Show Guy says he'll time us! Places!

[*Exeunt. A brief pause, then,* JESS *enters and signals to Puppet Show Guy.*]

JESS: [*To the wings.*] And GO!

[*At high speed, the actors reenact the highlights of* Hamlet, *matching the original staging and diction.*]

J/HAMLET: "O that this too too solid flesh would melt.

D/HORATIO: My lord, I think I saw your father yesternight.

J/HAMLET: Would the night were come.

[ADAM *enters as* GHOST, *wearing the ghost helmet and a sign that reads 'BOO.'*]

A/GHOST: Mark me!

J/HAMLET: Something is rotten in the state of Denmark.

A/GHOST: Revenge my murther.

D/HORATIO: My lord, this is strange.

J/HAMLET: Well, there are more things in heaven and earth so piss off! [*Slaps* DANIEL.]

[ADAM *dons the wig to become* OPHELIA.]

J/HAMLET: To be or not to be, that is the—

A/OPHELIA: Good my lord!

J/HAMLET: Get thee to a nunnery!

A/OPHELIA: [*Screams.*] Aaaaaaagh!

[JESS *uses his hands as puppets.*]

J/HAMLET: Now, speak the speech trippingly on the tongue.

[ADAM *puts the wig over his chin for a beard, and holds crown to head to become* CLAUDIUS.]

A/CLAUDIUS: Give o'er the play.

J/HAMLET: I'll take the ghost's word for a thousand pound. Now, mother, what's the matter?

A/GERTRUDE: Thou wilt not murther me. Help!

D/POLONIUS: Help! Help!

J/HAMLET: How now, a rat!

[*J/HAMLET throws his hat at* D/POLONIUS, *'killing' him.*]

    Dead for a ducat, dead.

D/LAERTES: Now, Hamlet, where's Polonius?

J/HAMLET: At supper.

D/LAERTES: Where?

J/HAMLET: Dead.

A/OPHELIA: [*Throws a tankard of water in her own face.*] Aaaaaaaa!

D/LAERTES: Sweet Ophelia!

J/HAMLET: [*Produces the rubber skull.*] Alas, poor Yorick! But soft, here comes the queen.

[D/LAERTES *kneels while* ADAM, *as* GERTRUDE, *flings Ophelia's corpse at* LAERTES.]

D/LAERTES: Lay her in the earth.

A/GERTRUDE: Sweets to the sweet. [*Flings flowers onto Ophelia's corpse.*]

D/LAERTES: Hold off the earth awhile.

[DANIEL *flings the corpse; it hits* ADAM *and knocks him to the floor.*]

J/HAMLET: It is I, Omelet the Cheese Danish!

[JESS *tosses the skull away over his shoulder.* DANIEL *deftly catches it.*]

D/LAERTES: The devil take thy soul.

J/HAMLET: Give us the foils.

[A/GERTRUDE *hands plastic swords to* J/HAMLET *and* D/LAERTES *who immediately stab each other.*]

D/LAERTES: One for me. O! I am slain! [*Dies.*]

A/GERTRUDE: [*Drinks from the goblet.*] O I am poisoned. [*Dies.*]

J/HAMLET: I follow thee. The rest is silence. [*Dies.*]"

[*Applause. They stand and bow.*]

JESS: [*To Puppet Guy, in the wings.*] Did we do it? [*Beat; then, to audience.*] Forty-seven seconds!

DANIEL: A new world's record!

ALL: Woo-hoo!

ADAM: [*After the cheers die down.*] Hey, do we have any time left?

DANIEL: Thirty seconds.

ADAM: Yes!

JESS: Very well! My friends, we shall do it—

ALL: *Faster!*

[*Exeunt. After a beat,* J/HAMLET, D/LAERTES *and* A/OPHELIA *enter running, each with a deadly prop. All simultaneously scream a line.*]

J/HAMLET: To be or not to be!

A/OPHELIA: [*Simultaneously.*] Aaaaaaaaaa!

D/LAERTES: [*Simultaneously.*] The devil take thy soul!

[*Each actor applies their instrument of death to themselves and dies. Pause, then all bounce up again for bows.* JESS *and* ADAM *exit.*]

DANIEL: [*Giddy.*] You've been such a fantastic audience, we're gonna do it . . . backward!

[JESS *and* ADAM *re-enter;* ADAM *staring at* DANIEL *incredulously.* DANIEL *lies down in his final death pose.* JESS *and* ADAM *follow his lead and assume the final death tableau.*]

ADAM: Wait, what about Puppet Show Guy?

DANIEL: [*Looks offstage.*] He just gave us a thumbs-up.

[*Pause. Then* JESS *sits up.*]

JESS: Be sure to listen for the Satanic messages.

[JESS *resumes his death pose. Pause. Then the backward encore begins, and sure enough, it is an exact reversal of the lines, movement, gestures, and blocking of the first encore, like a video played backward. The actors even* run *backward.*]

J/HAMLET: Silence is rest the. Thee follow I.

[J/HAMLET *and* D/LAERTES *bounce up to their feet and begin running backward with swords sticking out of their torsos.*]

A/GERTRUDE: Paul is dead!

D/LAERTES: Slain am I O!

J/HAMLET: Foils the us give. Dane the Hamlet, I is this.

[D/LAERTES *and* J/HAMLET, *running backward, extract the plastic swords from each other's torsos and deftly hand them to* A/GERTRUDE *who hurls them into the wings.*]

D/LAERTES: Earth the off hold. [*Throws flowers to* A/GERTRUDE.]

A/GERTRUDE: Sweets the to sweet.

[DANIEL *tosses the corpse to* ADAM, *who hurls it into the wings.*]

D/LAERTES: Earth the in her lay.

J/HAMLET: Queen the comes here.

[D/LAERTES *tosses the rubber skull over* J/HAMLET's *shoulder. It lands smoothly in his hand.*]

J/HAMLET: Yorick poor, alas!

D/LAERTES: Ophelia sweet!

A/OPHELIA: [*Spits a mouthful of water into the tankard, spraying part of the front row in the process, then screams backward.*] aaaaaaaAAAAAA!

D/LAERTES: Father my is where?

J/HAMLET: Dead. Ducat a for dead.

D/POLONIUS: Help!

A/GERTRUDE: Help! Me murder not wilt thou. Do thou wilt what.

[*J/HAMLET spins A/GERTRUDE in a backward pirouette.*]

J/HAMLET: Matter the what's, mother now?

D/POLONIUS: Rises king the!

[*As DANIEL runs past, backward, he hurls OPHELIA's wig into the air.*]

J/HAMLET: Tongue the on trippingly speech the speak.

[*ADAM spins to change character to OPHELIA as the wig lands on his head.*]

A/OPHELIA: aaaaaaaaAAA!

J/HAMLET: Nunnery a to thee get!

A/OPHELIA: Lord my good.

J/HAMLET: Be to not or be to. Off piss, Horatio, earth and heaven in things more are there!

D/HORATIO: Strange is this, lord my.

[*A/GHOST produces the 'BOO' sign from first encore, but holds it upside-down so it seems to spell 'OOB' but with a backward 'B.'*]

A/GHOST: Oob!

J/HAMLET: Denmark of state the in rotten is something.

D/HORATIO: Yesternight father your saw I think I, Lord my.

J/HAMLET: Melt would flesh solid too too this that—

ALL: O! You thank!!

[*All bow and exit. Blackout. Curtain call.*]

THE END